Spiritually Parenting *Your* Preschooler

C. Hope Flinchbaugh

SPIRITUALLY PARENTING YOUR PRESCHOOLER
by C. Hope Flinchbaugh
Published by Charisma House
A part of Strang Communications Company
600 Rinehart Road
Lake Mary, Florida 32746
www.charismahouse.com

Cover design by Judith McKittrick

Incidents and persons portrayed in this book are based on fact. Some names, places and any identifying details may have been changed and altered to protect the privacy and anonymity of the individuals to whom they refer. Any similarity between the names and stories of individuals known to readers is coincidental and not intentioned.

Library of Congress Cataloging-in-Publication Data

Flinchbaugh, C. Hope
Spiritually parenting your preschooler / C. Hope Flinchbaugh.
p. cm.
ISBN 0-88419-971-1 (trade paper)
1. Preschool children--Religious life. 2. Child rearing--Religious aspects--Christianity. I. Title
BV4529.F57 2003
248.8'45--dc21
2003007494

03 04 05 06 87654321
Printed in the United States of America

Dedication

For endless tasks of gentle patience–
Sticky fingers,
Dirty diapers,
Gerber feedings,
Teary nights,
Messy faces.
For the memories that belong only to us–
Hikes in the fall,
The Christmas donkey,
Pouring pajama praise parties,
Giggling preschoolers on piggyback,
Bunk bed prayers.
For the love that grows stronger between us–
The lake that reflects the green in your eyes,
Your whistle when you walk in the door after work,
Your guitar strums that fill our house,
Back cracks and neck rubs,
For teamwork and friendship,
I dedicate this book to my husband and my friend,
Scott Flinchbaugh.

Contents

Introduction

I promise you that this book is not about historical parenting. But before we delve into twenty-first-century parenting, let's look at the rocking-chair prayers of Mary Ball Washington—prayers that shaped and molded the man we honor now as the founding father of our nation.

On the day that young George left home to begin a life of service to his country, he knelt before his mother's rocking chair. Mary Ball Washington prayed over her son's future, much the same way she had been praying for George from that chair since he was an infant. I wonder what was going through her mind and what emotions washed over her soul as she said that last rocking-chair prayer.

After praying, Mary told her son, "Remember that God only is our sure trust. To Him, I commend you. My son, neglect not the duty of secret prayer."

During the next few years of combat, George Washington distinguished himself in battle during the French and Indian War. He became well known as the man who would not die. It is documented from several sources that four musket balls passed through his coat and two horses were shot out from under him, yet he never died.

Washington later credited his mother's prayers as the reason for his survival during many crises and several massacres in the British campaigns that followed.

An old venerable Indian chief went to battle to see the one he called "the young warrior of the great battle." Later, the chief said, "Our rifles were leveled, rifles which, but for him, knew not how to miss…a power mightier far than we shielded him from harm. He cannot die in battle."

Young George Washington had so impressed this chief that the Indian leader prophesied to his tribe, "Listen! The Great

Spirit protects that man and guides his destinies—he will become the chief of nations, and a people yet unborn will hail him as the founder of a mighty empire."[1] No wonder it is said that the hand that rocks the cradle rules the world.

Augustine and Mary Ball Washington did not have Fisher Price learning toys, day-care centers or Sesame Street videos to help them raise their little ones. This family of eight children had fewer helps and options than we do today, yet somehow they managed to find what Jesus called the "pearl of great price," so valuable that when found, one would sell all he had to get that one pearl. With God's help, within these pages you will find some of His most valuable, hidden pearls for spiritually parenting your preschooler in the twenty-first century.

What a great heritage Mary Ball Washington gave us all from her rocking chair! And how honored we are to have the same opportunity to give our children a rich birthright of a loving parent's rocking-chair prayers!

I remember the day our three preschoolers had totally exasperated me, and I looked up to the ceiling, hoping God could see down through it, and asked, "Is it really possible to actually walk in the Spirit with three wild preschoolers in the house?"

From that day on, walking in the Spirit with three preschoolers became my heart's pursuit. I would wake up in the morning—often in my recliner with my baby still in my arms—and say to God, "OK, it's a new day today. Help me, God, to walk in the Spirit." (Other days I was so exhausted that I would pray just to stay out of sin until Daddy got home from work so that I could take a nap for an hour.)

Please come and read with me. Bring this book to the park bench as your children play or to your lap as you feed your baby. (If you're like me, with more than one preschooler, you may want to put the book in the magazine rack in the bathroom!) Let's explore the wild, crazy days of preschool "adventures" and stretch our attention to hear the heart of God amid the clamor of preschool parenting.

1 Tag-Team Parenting

I'm writing this chapter on a night when I would really rather stand on top of the roof of my house and scream! You know, the night when Daddy's out of town on a hunting trip and Mom gets to run the whole show. (My hat is off and my head is bowed in prayer for single parents who do this 24/7. Keep reading, single parents; there's something for you here, too!)

Eighteen-month-old Judah got up from her nap on the wrong side of the crib today—could be because she has a cold. She worked herself into a frenzy until I had to get the nasal aspirator and clear her nose. She could breathe easier, but it certainly didn't improve her crying spell. So, I carried howling Judah on my hip, doing my best to sort out the frozen fish on a metal tray and pour the peas into the pan for supper.

Boom, Boom, Boom

About that time my three-year-old, Eden, decided to play our family's favorite praise tape (you know, the one with all the drums and only one slow song on the whole tape). Johnathan, my five-year-old, grabbed the metal mixing bowl and wooden spoon and beat the thing until I could feel my hair standing on end.

"Johnathan," I called out to him from the kitchen. Yeah, right, he's gonna hear me calling with the boom, boom, boom and Eden doing ring-around-the-rosy and somersaults all over the living room floor. OK, so I yelled. "JOHNATHAN!"

Our eyes met (always a good sign). "STOP!" (I've always found with preschoolers that short commands beat long explanations hands-down.)

Supper was still frozen, sitting on the counter. Baby Judah

was howling, the boom box still booming. Eden was still flipping, and Johnathan was a bit perturbed with Mom for shutting down his creativity on the "drums."

Time to pray—quickly

I took a break. You know the feeling. The one where you know you'd better pray—quickly. I sat down with still crying Judah in my lap and prayed, "Lord, please give me the grace that I need to cook supper and take care of these children while their daddy's away." It was a short prayer, but I felt reconnected with God.

It's tempting during these hairy times to allow the needs of the children to push me through the day. When things get hairy, I've learned that I'll lose my own personal peace unless I stop what I'm doing, even if the baby is still howling, and pray. Then I proceed from that place of momentary peace and connection with God to meet the next demand.

I got up from my prayer chair and looked out my living room window to see two teenage girls walking down the street. I had prayed for this opportunity, so I grabbed the church announcement, still carrying the baby, and walked out to meet them. Judah quit howling as soon as I stepped outside. (I'll have to remember that trick.) I invited both girls to the youth group event at my church the following Saturday night. It's hard to believe God could fit one more thing into my schedule tonight.

Back inside, I put on one of Judah's favorite Quigley's Village videotapes. It rescued me from her clinging howls long enough to get the oven and burners going for supper.

PEAS ON AIRPLANES

Supper commenced, and Eden started to cry (right about the time that all she had left on her plate were her peas), complaining that her leg hurt and she couldn't eat.

Judah yelled and pointed. She wanted the catsup.

My five-year-old, Johnathan, saw me doing airplanes with the girls' peas and begged, "Mommy, make me an airplane." Easier said than done.

The phone rang while I was trying to do two "airplanes" at once to get my daughters to eat their peas. "Show baby Judah how to eat her peas, Eden."

"Hello...Flinchbaughs," I answered briskly, ready to pour out the day's events on some poor family member or friend.

"Hello, this is Robin So-and-so, the editor for the preschooler's Sunday school curriculum." (So much for the peas.)

"Oh, hi," I answered weakly, a little deflated that I wasn't going to get to spill my tall tale and a little embarrassed at my brisk phone greeting. I decided to be honest. I figured I had never met the lady before, and once she heard my kids in the background she'd never ask me to write for her preschool paper, anyway.

"Well, I have a house full of preschoolers right now, three of them...five, three and eighteen months." (By now all three were crying.)

"Oh, I called at a bad time."

I tried to stay optimistic. "It's OK. I was just trying to get my girls to eat their peas on airplanes, and my five-year-old son... can you hold on?"

"Sure," she answered.

Johnathan was crying his eyes out—really out of character for him. "What's the matter?"

"The airplane you made me doesn't work."

"Look, this is an important phone call. I'll make a new one as soon as I get off. OK?"

"OK," he said, tears streaming down his face.

"Be at peace, Son," I said, putting my hand on his head. It worked. Wow!

Speak peace in the storm

Let me take a break in this story to interject a thought. When the disciples were terrified of drowning during the storm on the lake, in their frenzied state they woke up Jesus, wondering if He really cared about them. *How can He just sleep when we're in the depths of despair?*

In response, Jesus stood up and said, "Peace, be still."

Sometimes our little ones are just as frenzied and "in the depths of despair" over their small trials. Like the disciples, they are amazed that we can just sleep through it all. On countless occasions during my preschool "storms," I have employed Jesus' words by laying my hand on my child's head or chest and just speaking the word, "Peace."

I even have the children lay their hands on their own chests and speak, "Peace." There is power in the words we speak, and that one little word carries a pack of power in our house.

Back to the story.

I started talking to the preschool editor again.

Eden yelled into the phone, "Mommy, will you get my shoes and socks on, I said!"

The baby toddled to the back door, "Outside, outside!"

I stopped my telephone conversation again to talk to each of them. "I'll put your shoes on (Eden), and I'll help you make a new airplane (Johnathan), and we'll go outside (baby Judah) as soon as I'm off the phone. OK?"

When I got back on the phone, I had to stifle a giggle when the editor asked me, "What do you do?"

She was serious. So I offered to write some preschool material for her publishing company's curriculum. In the end, she took my name and address. I'm still wondering if she put that information in her "Possible Preschool Writer" file or her "Stay Away From This Author" file.

Baths and oatmeal

After cleaning up the supper dishes and sweeping the floors, I headed to the bathroom to give baths. I usually try to squeeze in cleaning the bathroom while I give my girls a bath. It's a good deal because they get to play until they're pink prunes, and I get a chore out of the way.

Johnathan suddenly acquired an enormous appetite. (I told him he should have eaten his peas at supper.) So he ate oatmeal—four packs of oatmeal. I'm trying to get him to be more independent, so I left the last packet on the counter for him to mix himself, and I left the milk on the table. I came out to the kitchen with squeaky-clean Judah in my arms. Johnathan was sitting on the floor with the broom and dustpan "cleaning up" scattered dry oatmeal.

"That's good you're cleaning it up, Johnathan," I said, trying to keep my optimism.

The plan was to get right back to Eden who was still in the tub.

Suddenly Johnathan let out a shriek. "Mom, LOOK!"

I turned and saw that Judah had climbed into her brother's chair and poured milk into his empty bowl. It was like that old meatball song everybody sang in grade school. It rolled off the table and onto the floor. And then our last milk supply—it was no more.

I grabbed Judah and quickly put her into her high chair before my clean baby became a smelly sour milk baby. I sent Johnathan back to the bathroom to check on Eden.

I promised the baby I would be back to give her a snack and left to get Eden out of the tub. I walked into the bathroom just in time to see Eden using the big green rinse cup to toss water over the edge of the tub. And just to make sure she got everything really clean, she dumped all of the liquid baby bath soap into the water.

Rolling Out the Red Carpet

So we gathered all the soapy, slimy toys, and I sloshed over the soaking wet, red bathroom rug to pull her out of the tub. I didn't ask her to, but she got a towel and tried to wipe up the mess. Hey, Mom was impressed.

I came out to give baby Judah her cereal to find Johnathan sitting at the table staring into space and the baby standing backward on top of her high chair tray.

"Johnathan, why didn't you call me?"

"I didn't see her."

Go figure.

I strapped that skinny little child into her high chair (which I had forgotten to do during the milk-spill episode) and started both of them on their snacks.

Gee, and Johnathan didn't even get his bath yet!

The bath rug was soaked. I couldn't leave it where it was, so I rolled it up and made a dash for the front porch. I flung the thing over the porch railing just as my husband pulled into the driveway with his dad and uncle.

"Hey, you're rolling out the red carpet for him, are you?" my father-in-law called out the window of his truck.

I thought, *I'm gonna roll some red carpet if he doesn't get in here and help me.* Of course, I didn't say that. I'm not like my children; I don't say the first thing that comes to mind (usually).

Wanting relief

I was glad that Daddy made it home in time to pray with the children before they slept. I didn't want to pray—not because I had lost my peace somewhere in the middle of the madness with the kids. Really, I didn't lose my peace until my husband came home.

Hey, it happens. Truth is, when he pulled in, I wanted relief, and I wanted someone to listen to my woes. A medal of honor or a red badge of courage would have been nice.

If given half the chance, most of us try to hold up our end of the ship until someone shows up who we know loves us enough to let us blow off steam about how tough we have it. If we're honest, we like to blame a lot of preschooler miseries on our partners, whether they're present at the time of trouble or not.

Yes, this is a book on preschoolers, but we parents are the ones who have to remain steady enough to raise them. And we won't raise them if we're worried about which parent is at fault for half the floors in the house being a disaster area.

FINDING VIRTUE

After the children were in bed, my husband, who was rested and suddenly enlightened by his trip away from it all, pointed out the virtues in each of our children.

"Now, Mommy," he said, his eyes smiling. "Each one of them was trying to do something good, and they just made a mess of it."

"Good?" I asked, rolling my eyes. "You wouldn't have thought it was *so good* if you had been here."

"Well, I know they made a mess, but listen. Johnathan was just trying to mix his own oatmeal. And Baby Judah was trying to help him by pouring the milk in the bowl. She just didn't know how to make it stop."

"And Eden? I guess you can find some virtue in her throwing cupfuls of water over the side of the tub? And don't forget, it wasn't just water. It was slippery, sudsy water. Do you know that she dumped all of the baby bath soap in the water?"

"I know. Maybe she saw a hair or something on the side of the tub and was trying to wash it away."

I didn't say it, but I really thought he was stretching it a bit there.

"She was just trying to clean like Mommy cleans the bathroom."

Hmmm. Didn't think of that.

Teamwork

Well, even so. Sometimes our little ones do things, and we can find no virtue in their actions at all.

Remember, it takes two to be a team. Teamwork? You bet. Even when Mom is away on a business trip, or Dad is gone hunting for a few days, you're still a team. The parent left alone with the children should continue to hold up the routines and standards set by the absent parent.

Single parent—I wish I could jump off this page and hug you. My heart goes out to parents who are all alone without the involvement of their child's other parent. But never forget that you are still part of a team—it's you and God in this thing together.

One single mother told me, "I want to share the wonder of it all (parenting) with my children's dad, but he doesn't want to be involved. I want him to share in the positives and negatives and to have his help as one of our children suffers the pain of an ear infection or a behavior pattern. Watching them grow is too wonderful to take in alone. When their dad doesn't ask about our children's well-being, it can be crushing. Then I have to deal with the resentment of having to do it all alone all day."

If this situation sounds pretty close to yours, ask God to surround you with people who can be a support system. Every parent needs someone to whom she or he can talk about parenting. Of course, every parent needs some time alone, too.

Sometimes single parents think, *This is my responsibility*, or *This is my lot in life*. But remember that you are teaming with God. Let Him help you set up a support base. It's OK to ask for help and to get support. Did someone you trust offer to help with the kids so you can get a break? God may have nudged them to offer to help. Take them up on it!

If at all possible, involve your own parents in your child's life. I know one single mom who takes her children to see her parents twice a week. If you're a single mom or dad without the help of your parents, look for a couple in your church or neighborhood who would be willing to become a part of your lives. Some retired couples may delight in a simple walk or a trip to the zoo. As your children spend time with these married couples, they will reap the benefit of seeing you relax and interact with members of the opposite sex.

If your children's other parent is involved in their lives, it is important to come up with a plan to work together for the children's benefit despite the differences between the two of you. You are no longer husband and wife, but the two of you will always be your children's mother and father. It may require great effort on your part to create a working parental relationship, but you can at least do your part and pray for the absent parent to do his as he sees your example. Here are some thoughts on teamwork for single parents:

1. "Out of the abundance of the heart the mouth speaks" (Matt. 12:34). If your child's other parent has been an irritation, you will talk about it with someone because "need" always finds a voice. Try to discuss these needs or problems when your child is not with you.

2. Don't argue with the absent parent over the telephone while the child is in the room.

3. Go the extra mile and ask God to give you kind things to say about the absent parent. Your children need to know that the absent parent loves them and that you are OK with that. Tell your child, "Mommy (or Daddy) loves you a lot. I'm glad you love your dad (or mom), too. You'll get to see him (or her) in a few days."

4. Don't allow your precious preschooler to be a prize to be given or taken away depending upon the absent parent's behavior. This is devastating to your child. Visitations with a good parent should continue on as regular a schedule as possible, and if worse comes to worse, financial issues should be settled in court—not in front of your child.

5. If you suspect your child is being abused, you should document the abuse and the dates of its occurrence. Ask neighbors or friends who are around the absent parent to document the times they have observed abusive behavior. Immediately seek counsel and withdraw your child from any situation that you are sure is abusive.

When Mom and Dad are opposites

Teamwork is the greatest when Mom and Dad are opposites.

Moms like to diaper the baby so that every hook and flap is even and perfect, while dads usually have a great sense of accomplishment in just remembering to stick a dry diaper on the baby now and then.

Moms tend to stock the diaper bag with a weekend's worth of diapers just to go to the grocery store, while dads feel it's enough just to grab the bottle and walk out the door. Remember that these differences are small, and the baby will thrive happily with either parent.

Moms and dads play differently, too. My husband gets on the floor almost every night and wrestles with his preschoolers. When he encouraged me to get in on the fun, I honestly tried. There was absolutely no thrill, fulfillment or bonding for me in wrestling on the floor.

I like holding them, reading to them and making cookies with them. Dad can have the floor.

When things get hairy (and they will), hold on to your peace. And hold on to your mate. You're a team, even when one person's not there physically. And that teamwork means everything.

JOURNAL TIME—WHAT'S THAT?

Have you read the introduction to this book yet? I talked about the rocking-chair prayers of George Washington's mother, Mary Ball Washington. You know, we would never know the prayers that President Washington and his mother prayed had he not written them down in his prayer diary.

King David also wrote down his prayers and his songs to God. In fact, David had a great sense of purpose in his writing. He didn't write just for his children, but also for the generations yet to come. Listen to David's heart:

> I will make Your name to be
> remembered in all generations;
> Therefore the people shall praise
> You forever and ever.
>
> —PSALM 45:17

David's vision for writing down his prayers and songs went

beyond just showing them to his immediate family. David foresaw the impact of his faith in God reverberating for the generations yet to come.

I want to invite you to take a few moments now to jot down a prayer you've prayed or to write down something you've learned about teamwork. Of course, there's no obligation to write a thing, but it will be great fun showing this book to your son or daughter one day when they're raising their preschoolers!

So we...will give You thanks forever;
We will show forth Your praise to all generations.

—Psalm 79:13

Father God, in Jesus' name I pray...

After reading this chapter, what one thing (or more) do you feel that you have been doing right?

What one change would you like to see in your home?

2 A Baby!

Scott and I were so ecstatic—a baby!

We got on two extensions of our telephone, sprawled across our bed and called all of our friends.

"Hello, Sarah. Is Will there, too? We want to talk to both of you."

"Hello, this is Will."

"We're going to have a baby," we chorused. Every one of our friends laughed and rejoiced and even squealed a little. We called just about everyone in our address book.

I watched my parents' faces as they opened an early anniversary card for them that I had signed, "Love, Baby Flinchbaugh." They were so happy!

The Barren Years

I was thirty-two before I was able to conceive and carry to full term. During those empty barren years, I longed to hold my own child, shedding many sorrowful tears of grief. (In retrospect, I have often thought, *If I had the money back from the all the pregnancy tests I bought throughout the years, I could pay for a semester of Johnathan's future college education.*)

God spoke to my heart one summer from Romans 4:18–20. It says, "Against all hope, *Abraham in hope believed* and so became the father of many nations" (NIV, emphasis added). He didn't consider his own body's physical limitations, and he never wavered at God's promise. He gave glory to God *before* his son was ever conceived. He was fully convinced that God was able to perform what He had promised.

Somehow, God dropped faith in my heart when I read those verses. I even wrote a song, which became kind of a faith statement for me, called "I Believe." I would like to share the words of that song with you right now.

You've given me Your promises,
You've given me Your Word.
For Your name is Faithful, Wonderful and True.
And I believe! I believe! I believe in You!
I remember Father Abraham
Didn't waver in unbelief.
And everything You've ever said will come true.
But glorifying You, his faith just grew.
For Your name is Faithful, Wonderful and True!
Giving glory! Glory! Glory to You!

One month after writing "I Believe," we conceived our first child.

A couple of my friends who had difficulty with carrying a child full term told me they were standing on the scripture in Malachi 3:10–11. God told His people that if they would tithe 10 percent of their income, "the vines in your fields will not cast their fruit" (NIV). Now, the Bible does specifically say "the vines in your fields," but because the Bible refers to the wife as a fruitful vine, some have applied this verse to their bodies as well.

Still other couples have felt God drawing them into the high calling of adopting children or helping to parent children on an interim basis through foster care. Whatever God's plans are for us as parents, it takes faith to receive these precious lives that God is entrusting to us.

Faith Becomes Sight

When I first became pregnant, it took a while for my mind to fathom the miracle of what was happening inside of me. One day, a dear friend squeezed me with delight all over her face and declared, "Just imagine! All that precious life is exploding inside of you, growing and forming."

I thought, *Hmmm. Really?*

Really! A real spirit being, capable of all the things I'm capable of. It wasn't until my abdomen finally began to round out that I was able to grasp visually the reality that I was really going to have a baby.

Adopting parents are usually thrilled when they receive the picture of the child they are about to adopt. But then there is the long wait that must be endured until what is "faith" becomes "sight."

Some parents feel God nudging their hearts to adopt, and I know of several parents to whom God had given dreams about the children they were to adopt. This is God's way of planting a seed in those parents' hearts, enabling them to carry their child, not in the womb, but in the Spirit through prayer and faith until the moment they bring that child home. Two of my friends named their daughters Faith because of the enormous journey of faith that they went on before they finally held their daughters in their arms.

CARRYING THE SPIRIT

I was thrilled to carry my baby. But what else was I carrying? Excitement? Worry? Fear? Joy?

I was keenly aware that what I carried in my spirit was transferring to my baby inside of me. If I was under stress during the daytime, sometimes I felt my large abdomen tense and harden.

At night, after we settled into bed, the baby worked to settle in with us. Scott felt the roundness of the child forming inside of me and delighted in the kick to his hand as he applied pressure at various points. I loved listening to his quiet prayers over our little one.

Adopting parents, may I make a suggestion? Why not place your hands over the womb of your spirit and pray for your child, too?

I felt particularly bonded with my baby when I sang. Sometimes I put a favorite song on our stereo or I sat at the piano and sang directly to God. I truly felt one with my Lord and my baby during those times. When Daddy was able to join me, the unity just increased. This kind of unity of spirit can happen with adopting parents, too. The God who calls us to adopt also knits our hearts even before we see each other. Prayer and worship always bring us closer to our children and to our children's Creator than anything else.

Does your baby partake of that same refreshing praise to God as Mommy does when she worships? You'd better believe it! Many expecting mothers have told me how their babies were unusually active during particularly strong times of worship at home or in church. I've experienced the same thing.

John leaped in Elizabeth's womb when Mary came to visit. Isn't that incredible? That particular story shows that John was spiritually sensitive while in the womb.

Jesus said that children's angels are always beholding the face of the Father. Psalm 139 says that God is there, hedging them in behind and before, knitting them together in the womb.

Praying for Baby

On the day I saw that little blue plus sign on the home pregnancy test, I began to do what my mother and father had done when they were expecting me—I prayed for my baby. My favorite way to pray is to pray scriptures with faith. Countless times I have read or quoted portions of Psalm 139 over my children. This is my paraphrased prayer over my babies:

> *Lord, You've searched and known my baby. You are familiar with every movement in the womb. You've hedged this baby in from behind and before—he is hemmed in by You, and I won't miscarry. Your hand is on my child, and I know it.*
>
> *You are creating my baby's innermost being. You are knitting him today inside my womb. God, I praise You for making my child so fearfully and wonderfully. I know that You see my baby. He is not hidden from You, but woven together by Your hand. Even now, Your eyes can see his unformed substance.*
>
> [This is my favorite part.] *In Your book You've written down a plan for every day that this baby will live. Help me as his mother always to flow with Your plans and not to hinder*

them by my own selfishness.

God, You are thinking about my baby all the time! And You are thinking about me, too. Lord, search my heart and test me. Look at my anxious thoughts and steer me into right thinking. If there's any way in me that's going to be a stumbling block to my parenting this child, please show me. I want to be corrected. And lead me in Your way, so that I can see things as You see them—with the perspective You have from heaven.

In Jesus' name, amen.

Usually by this time I was crying tears of joy, worshiping and thanking God. They were the grateful tears of a once barren woman.

HAVE THE BABY—SAFELY

Even women of great faith in God can grow anxious about delivery.

Sometimes the sight of a pregnant woman is all it takes for a flock of women to gather with great excitement to share their collection of wild and even horrifying birth stories. Baby showers are particularly famous for these "wives' tales" that leave the guests *oohing* and *aahing* while the new mother stands wide-eyed with a new stack of fears to deal with.

I was so thankful when a friend of mine opened my first baby shower with a prayer that God would cause each of us to be sensitive not to share birthing stories that weren't edifying.

On the other side of the coin, there are some people who tell glorious birthing stories declaring that we are free from the curse of the law so we should be free from pain in childbirth. The stories are wonderful to listen to—unless the storytellers openly say or imply that a birth can be medication free and pain free if only the expecting couple is "spiritual enough."

By the time I was ready to deliver my third baby, I had heard some of these effortless birthing stories. Often the women who received the highest acclaim in bearing a child (as if birthing were a competition) were those who gave birth in bathtubs at home. I began to worry that I needed to be a super mom and have this third child with no pain medication, no episiotomy and no troubles. (I had no high aspirations, however, of giving birth in a bathtub.)

A friend of mine who is an administrator of a Christian school wisely advised me, "Look, the object here is to have the baby and to have it safely." Those few words put me at peace. I decided that birthing my baby was a big enough task in itself.

Please understand, I am not criticizing those who had a birthing process that was either horrifying or glorifying, in the hospital or at home. I just want to put my arms around expecting parents and say what my friend said to me—the object here is to have the baby and have it safely.

I believed for my own safety as well. I staked my claim in 1 Timothy 2:15, which says, "Nevertheless she will be saved in childbearing if they continue in faith, love, and holiness, with self-control."

And do keep a sense of humor about the whole thing so that your heart will not get heavy or impatient. Toward the end of my pregnancy with my third child, I set my cassette alarm clock to go off with the gospel soul song that blared out, "I've been delivered!" I woke up smiling every morning with that song and that prayer on my lips. It kept the humor between Scott and me on mornings when I really felt like being nasty instead of nice.

Preparing for Birth

I would like to say a word to families expecting their second (or maybe eighth) child. When I was carrying my third child, Judah Hope, I wondered how I could possibly love the third child as much as my first two. But you know, the love is there, and it grows and builds with each feeding, bath and snuggle.

While waiting for delivery, there are many things you can do for your baby as he grows inside of you. Eat what is healthy, rest when your body tells you to, and prepare in prayer. Sing to your child, pray for your child, speak verses of Scripture to him or her, and just enjoy the honor of bringing new life into the world.

> Thine eyes have seen my unformed substance;
> And in Thy book they were all written,
> The days that were ordained for me,
> When as yet there was not one of them.
>
> —PSALM 139:16, NAS

God knows the days ordained for each person, so I prayed that my baby would come forth on a given day, the day God ordained for him or her to be born.

A dear friend of mine was with me during my third delivery. God put it on her heart to be there, and although I'm a very private person, I knew it was of God that she joined us in this most intimate experience. This friend was a gift from God to me that day, and her presence in the delivery room gave my husband breaks to go for food or make phone calls. I found that even though this was my third delivery, she was a much-needed rock of support to me throughout the birth.

My friend is a great photographer, and I was thrilled when she later showed me pictures of my newborn before the blue umbilical cord was cut.

Just as every child is different, every child's birth experience is different, too. Enjoy the privilege of bringing life into the world, and shut out all the "fear stories" and "glory stories" that well-meaning people sometimes push on pregnant women. Trust God to gladly lead you safely through each phase of delivery.

ESTABLISHING TRUST

Parents of children ages preborn to two have an awesome opportunity to build their child's emotional foundation. According to the teachings of John and Paula Sandford of Elijah House Ministry, trust is the fundamental building foundation of all human relationships, and it is the first stage of emotional development in children.

Psalm 22:9 says, "You brought me out of the womb; you made me trust in you even at my mother's breast" (NIV).

If a parent picks up his baby when she cries, that child learns to feel that she can have an effect in this world, that she has a voice and it will be heard. Although a baby may eventually give up crying if she's not picked up, she will learn that her voice will not make a difference.

At first, before the parent begins to discern the cry of his child, it can be confusing for the infant. Perhaps the child cries because she needs a diaper change, but the parent assumes the baby is hungry and tries to feed her instead. These are small bumps on the road to establishing the emotional haven of trust that every child needs.

Affectionate touch will build basic trust in the baby and a strength of spirit that will help her to open her heart to people and to life itself.

The Sandford's Elijah House teachings emphasize that a child whose parent comes for her when she cries and who experiences affectionate touch from both parents not only develops the sense that, "I'm OK, I'm loved," but also develops the courage to venture out to try new things and the resilience to bounce back after a difficulty.

Is Three a Crowd?

When baby Judah Hope was born, I wondered how life would change with three preschool children in the house. The conflict that arose for me was how to find actual time to spend with my third child. Once again I had two in diapers, and the demands of just feeding, bathing and dressing them all took gobs of time.

One day, right after Judah was born, I carried the laundry upstairs right past her playpen. I could barely see over the top of the laundry basket—I tripped over the toys and stubbed my toe on the playpen.

"Ehh!" My little one called me from the blue playpen, her big eyes following my movement past her. It was her baby way of saying, "Hey Mom, I'm here."

Bless her heart, her tiny uncoordinated body wouldn't let her reach out her arms to be held. For now, her little "ehh" was all she could muster. She contented herself and let me pass by her once again.

Is this the plight of the third child? I wondered.

The end of the day was like the end of every other day. Clear the table, pack the lunch, tidy cluttered rooms, read Bible stories, give baths, put one last clean diaper on two bottoms, give snacks, brush teeth and send off to bed. The routine seemed unending with no breaks.

"I feel so bad," I told my husband. "I don't have time for Judah like I did the other two. I don't get to just sit down and nurse her and enjoy her. I have to nurse her while correcting the other two, rescuing my makeup from their hot little hands, answering the door or kissing boo-boos. It's so hard for her to just have Mommy."

My husband looked at me thoughtfully, never in a hurry to respond to my woes with an immediate answer.

I was in tears.

"Just be there for her when she needs you," he finally said.

"When she needs me?" I asked.

"Make sure that when she needs you, you respond to her. God will take care of the rest."

I've hung on to that, and although I've failed sometimes, my husband's words have come back to me again and again.

IN CLOSING...

When you've read the last page of this book, the most important part of it for you (in retrospect) will probably not be so much the words you've read as the words you've written in the journal section at the end of each chapter.

Perhaps you are not pregnant at the time of this reading. Or maybe you're in the "believing" or planning stage for your new baby. Wherever you are in your life with preschoolers, be sure to write down your heart's prayer during this special season in your life.

Journal Time

> You brought me out of the womb; you made me trust in you even at my mother's breast.
>
> —PSALM 22:9, NIV

Father God, in Jesus' name I pray...

What things did the Holy Spirit assure you that you are doing right?

What areas in parenting your infant did the Holy Spirit nudge you to change?

3 Offering Godly Images to Our Children

Remember this commandment? "You shall not make for yourself any carved image" (Exod. 20:4). Whew! At least that's one commandment we're not likely to break. But what types of images do we offer to our children in our homes? What mental pictures are imprinted on their minds? Cartoon characters? Movie stars? Sports figures? Jesus?

When my husband and I brought each of our little ones home from the hospital, we had a keen awareness that our baby's mind was like a blank page. What is pictured there now is a collection of what we have put in front of them.

Guard the Images

As parents, we set images before our children all the time. Mental pictures from television, movies, computers, books and songs materialize in the thoughts of our children every day. God created those little eyes and minds to record and store information, so part of our job as parents is to guard carefully the images and pictures set before our children's eyes and ears.

When my husband and I were first married, we taped a little three-by-five-inch index card to our television set that said, "I will set no worthless [unclean] thing before my eyes" (Ps. 101:3, NAS). As a couple, we wanted God's Holy Spirit to lead us through His Word to understand what images are worthy and clean to put before our eyes.

One of the blessings of living in our high-tech society is that we have access to so many godly teaching materials. Instead of paying monthly TV cable bills, my husband and I choose to purchase godly movies, music and books for our children.

Unlike adults, children love repetition. They can sit down and watch the same movie or have the same story read to them again and again.

Hug the Bible

The first book a Christian parent wants to read to their child is the Bible. I like to turn to the page in their picture Bible where Jesus is hugging the little boy and say, "I love Jesus." I actually kiss the picture of Jesus. It doesn't take long until baby wants to kiss Jesus, too!

In another Bible storybook, I turn to the picture of Jesus holding little children on His lap and, using hand motions, I sing, "Jesus Loves Me." This way my child has a visual picture of Jesus, a sense of physical touch or contact with Him and a catchy tune to associate with the picture. Most importantly, she sees that Jesus is very special to Mommy and Daddy.

Sometimes, while holding my baby on my lap, I get out my own Bible. I hug my Bible enthusiastically and kiss it and tell them, "I love the Bible." After showing my love for my Bible, I let the baby feel the shiny edges of the pages and smell the leather. I love it when they're cutting teeth and decide to bite it! I can hear them testifying as an adult, "I cut my teeth on the Word of God!"

Last year I took all three of my preschoolers into a Christian high school child development class. I was sharing this concept of hugging the Bible with a room full of teenagers when ten-month-old Judah grabbed the Bible out of my hand and hugged it, perfectly demonstrating her early love for the Word of God.

Of course, your little one's image of Mom or Dad reading that precious book will remain with them always. As a former preschooler of Christian parents, I can tell you today that thirty-five years ago my mother used a leatherbound red Bible with a red satin bookmark, which stuck out at the bottom. My dad, an ordained pastor, had several Bibles. He gave me the one he received at his ordination, and it is a treasure to me.

HIYA! HIYA!

Our children watched *The Donut Man on Tour* video from the time they were old enough to sit up in their little swing seat. It's an older video, and I wasn't very impressed with it at first. But my husband immediately saw its value and played it a couple of times each week.

Daddy and babies sat glued to the lively images and music. Before they could walk, our babies waved "hiya-hiya" branches. (I cut the branches off one of my fake house plants so they'd have a "palm branch" to praise Jesus with.) And as soon as they started walking, they toddled around in circles to the upbeat praise music.

GIANT FAITH IN ACTION

The story of David and Goliath is Johnathan's favorite story. I have pictures of Johnathan at two years of age covered with plastic armor, flattened on the floor by David's imaginary stone and slingshot. About a year later, I recorded home videos of him playing the part of David, swirling the sling around and around toward Daddy who crashed to the ground when Johnathan shouted, "You fight me with a spear and a sword, but I fight you in the name of the Lord of Hosts!" (By the way, he memorized that line by watching the Donut Man.)

One day when Johnathan was two, he applied the David and Goliath story in a very real way. He was outside when our neighbors' huge dog bounded out of their house and headed straight toward little Johnathan. My husband was there, ready to step in as needed. Johnathan's eyes widened as he watched that dog running straight for him.

In a flash, Johnathan raised his right arm and began twirling and slinging imaginary stones at that dog over and over again. Suddenly, the dog stopped within five feet of Johnathan, cocked its head sideways and looked at him like, "What are you doing, little kid?" At that moment, the owner called the dog, and it turned and walked away.

Although this incident was funny for my husband to observe, Johnathan's faith was truly strengthened. He took what little faith he had and used it. It worked!

Children Without Shoes

Sometimes our children need help discerning even the good images they see. I remember one day when Johnathan, about three years old, refused to put his shoes on.

"Mommy, I can't put my shoes on."

"Why not?"

"Because Jesus only takes up children without any shoes on," he explained.

"What do you mean, Jesus only takes up children without shoes on?" I asked. "Jesus loves all the children."

"Yeah, but only the ones without shoes on get to go up with Him. Remember? It's in the Bible."

Finally it clicked. Johnathan was referring to that familiar Bible picture of Jesus taking all the little children on His lap—and all of them had their shoes *off!*

"Mommy, That's Evil"

All three of our children collectively have not watched as many as fifteen hours of cartoons in their whole lives.

Once in a while I've exposed them to short clips of commercials or cartoons. Three-year-old Eden usually walks out of the room, totally disinterested. Five-year-old Johnathan is much more intrigued with animation. Still, almost every time he'll discern something evil and say, "Mommy, that's evil," or "Turn it off."

Because we don't have cable, they've rarely seen the big yellow bird, the blue dog or the big purple dinosaur. Twice I rented videos for them with these characters just so they could communicate intelligently about them with their peers.

We don't declare all of those programs as sinful. We just haven't needed their input in raising our children. Please understand that I am not sharing what we do as a family as a basis for what all parents should do. I am suggesting that we carefully and intentionally place healthy, moral, godly "images" before our children and not allow our television set or well-meaning relatives decide what is best for our child to view.

PRAYER FOR ELMO'S BATH

It's funny how "uncartooned" kids relate to cartoon characters. I was in the book section of Wal-Mart, looking for flash cards and fun workbooks for my children. I had the girls with me. Three-year-old Eden reached out and picked up a Sesame Street board book. She turned to a page where Elmo was taking a bath and began to "read."

"And Lord, I pray right now that I'll be able to take a bath. And I pray for...OK, you can take a bath now."

That may be the first time Elmo's bath was ever prayed over! Of course, five minutes later Eden let the whole store know that she did not want to be put back in the shopping cart. Isn't that the way it is with children? One moment you're warmed by their innocent perspectives, and the next you're correcting their selfish behavior!

HEROES

When I taught in day care, I daily watched preschoolers who were totally surrounded with cartoons and cartoon paraphernalia. They proudly displayed sneakers, book bags, shirts and underwear decorated with whatever cartoon "heroes" were new at the time. During playtime they acted out the cartoons they'd seen on television. This would often result in "time-outs" in a little chair because most of their heroes destroyed everything around them.

I remember a three-year-old who literally threw chairs at his day-care teacher because he'd seen a cartoon character throw chairs on television. For the safety of everyone, that teacher had to ask the parents not to allow him to watch that particular show anymore.

Enough of that—I really don't like negative stories, and I don't think there's much to learn there apart from a warning, "Don't do this." Please allow me to share a few personal stories of the positive impact of placing godly images in front of your children. I'm sure you have a story or two to tell along this line as well.

Scott and I want our children's heroes to be characters from the Bible. In my journal I have recorded a time when three-year-old Johnathan and his cousin Heather were playing.

"God is talking to us," Johnathan said excitedly. "Come on, let's go!"

He zoomed over to the front door and fell on his knees. He bowed down on the ground saying, "We bow down to worship Jesus because we love Him."

He and Heather ran around the living room shouting, "I'm healed; I'm all better!" Then they went back to the door for a repeat. They pretended to hug Jesus, each one saying, "I love You, Jesus!"

Johnathan spun around in the center of the floor saying, "Jesus is taking us to heaven." Next he repeated the whole thing, trying to get everyone who was watching involved.

I said, "You'll have to tell me what you see up in heaven—when you get back."

He looked at me as if I just fell off a turnip truck. "*Jesus* is in heaven."

"Of course," I answered. What was Mommy thinking?

Images of the Father Help the Fatherless

Displaying images of God is especially important to single-parent families. I know one single mom who really battles a fear that her children will not turn out perfectly because they don't have a father figure 24/7.

Because their father is rarely in their lives, she tells her three-year-old, "Daddy's heart is sick. Let's pray for Daddy."

Her three-year-old prays, "Jesus, heal Daddy's heart and bring him back to me."

This mother says that watching her daughter's heartbreak hurts more than one thousand rejections toward herself. Unfortunately, it's becoming increasingly common for dads to abandon both their children's lives and their responsibility toward their children. The world calls these fathers "deadbeat dads." I prefer to call them prodigals that Jesus is reaching for.

For this family, the painting by Ron DiCianni, which shows Jesus embracing the prodigal son, may be a wonderful image for the three-year-old daughter. The painting is a visual hope that Jesus can heal Daddy's heart and that He is listening to her prayers.

ACTING OUT IMAGES IN PLAY

If children are presented with images of God, they will act out those images in their imaginary play. Sometimes I see Johnathan and Eden in the backyard playing "Jesus." Eden nails Johnathan to the shed (the cross). She'll announce, "I'm a mean soldier."

Johnathan likes the next part. He gets the round turtle shell lid from the sandbox and props it up beside the sliding board. Then he "rolls the stone away," and the two of them run around the yard shouting, "Jesus is alive, hallelujah! He's alive!"

I giggle to myself sometimes, wondering how many neighbors they've witnessed to in their play times. (The euphoria ends when I hear them arguing just as loudly over a particular swing or yard toy.)

I'm not trying to label all television as sinful. Television programming just doesn't produce the quality or the quantity of fruit that biblical training produces. And it's important that we don't just keep the bad stuff away from them. As Christian parents, we need to make a genuine effort to offer our children godly images in books, videos, Christian crafts and music. It's our job to fill their impressionable imaginations with images of God.

Whenever I get "stuck" in figuring out how to parent my child, I look for Bible stories that may minister to me or to my child.

Bible Stories Impact Preschoolers

Why is it that two- and three-year-olds delight in stashing things in secret places? Everything from dirty diapers to unwanted vegetables rot in some dark hole until fumes from their decomposition send us scrambling to uncover last month's hidden sin.

With our two-year-old Judah, it has always been vitamins. She doesn't like the taste of them, so she stashes them in her secret hiding spots all over the house. One night her daddy gave her a vitamin and told her to take it. He sweetly and convincingly persuaded her to take it into her tiny hand. She's quite the daddy's girl, and she smiled reassuringly while he walked away into the kitchen. She watched him leave, and then, unaware that I was watching her, as quickly as her little legs would go, she scooted into her bedroom. After looking around to be sure no one was watching, she did a hook shot with that vitamin, ricocheting it off the wall as she threw it behind the dresser. Pleased that it made the mark, she turned around and walked back out to the living room. I turned my head and howled, then composed myself and told my husband what happened. He made her dig it out and dust it off, and she ate it anyway.

She had that same expression on her face as she did when we first offered her Gerber vegetables. It was a "don't feed me anymore of that green stuff" look where she turned her head sideways, buttoned up those lips and, out of the corner of her eye, dared us to try to make her eat it.

Judah's vitamins fall out of her car seat when I pull the tray up; they've been found in her shoes, in the tissue box, between the couch cushions and in the trash can. Not only does she hide vitamins, but she also enjoys hiding herself whenever she's called. I wondered if we'd ever break the "hiding habit." Where can a parent turn when a child continues misbehaving?

I kept thinking, *She's not getting as many Bible stories as the older two did.* I need to read more of the Word to her.

So I took a shot at reading more Bible stories. I tried the one about Jesus feeding the five thousand (Judah would gladly give Jesus her fish and bread if it meant she didn't have to eat it), David and Goliath (I wonder if she imagined slinging vitamins instead of stones) and God creating the world.

Judah would impatiently listen to my story choice and always ask for the Jonah story. I was thinking, *Jonah?* Over and over I would read Jonah from two or three different storybooks she found. After about two weeks of Jonah, Judah looked up at me one day while we were on page five and said, "He hidin'."

Lights. More lights. A sonic boom.

HIDING! That's it! I suddenly felt transformed from "Super Bomb" to "Super Mom!" I went for it!

"That's right. Jonah's hiding. Does God see Jonah?"

Judah nodded her little head. "Jonah should obey God. He shouldn't hide when God calls him."

Well, God ministered this story to Judah by His Holy Spirit. I didn't understand why she liked this particular story read to her over and over again. I was certainly tiring of Jonah. But God was ministering His life into my little girl, and when she showed me what that story meant to her, my trust in God soared.

And the vitamins? Well, she seems to be doing better, but let's just say I haven't cleaned behind her dresser for a while.

Whenever we call her, and Judah chooses to hide, all we have to do is say, "Could Jonah hide from God?" And eventually she crawls out of some dark hole grinning in obedient triumph. I love it! The Word works!

IN CLOSING...

Has the Holy Spirit nudged you or smiled over you while reading this chapter on offering godly images to our children? Is there a prayer that came to your heart as you read? If by some miracle the house is quiet, why not take a moment to write it down?

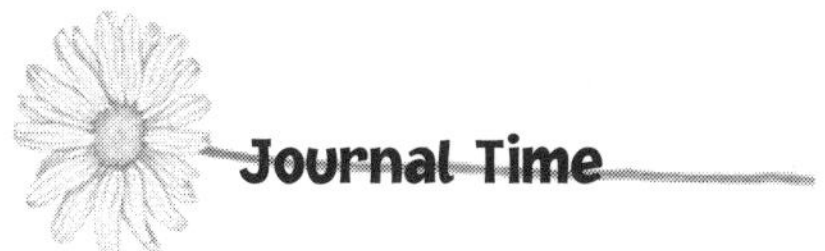

> I will set no worthless [unclean] thing before my eyes.
>
> —PSALM 101:3, NAS

Father God, in Jesus' name I pray...

What specific "godly images"—specific books, videos, television programs and other tools—have you incorporated into your family's life to help your children learn about God?

While you were reading this chapter, did the Holy Spirit speak to your heart about making changes in the "images" presented in your house? What were they?

4 Declare a Pajama Praise Party!

David mentions the word *praise* more than 125 times in the Book of Psalms—the number varies depending on which version you are reading. David knew how to pray and sing about the darkest dungeons of despair, but he also knew how to praise his God. In fact, if someone is looking for the power of positive thinking, praise will definitely get him there.

In sharing this chapter, I'm opening our living room windows to let you peek into some precious times we've shared as a family. But our family's way of worshiping God is far from being the only way. It's my hope that reading this chapter will be the spark that lights a unique and extraordinary fire for praise and worship in your home. In fact, let's pause right now to talk to God about you and your special family.

Father God, I ask in Jesus' name that Your presence will rest upon this precious parent and their family. May they hear Your wonderful voice as they read this chapter about our praises to You from our little home. Come closer, Lord, closer and closer until they feel Your breath upon their cheek and they know that You have spoken. Thanks, God.

A Weekly Balance, Physically and Spiritually

We really don't have a specific time set aside to worship God as a family. We use our instruments and cassette tapes to praise God all through the week. Once in a while we miss a day or two. Other times we'll praise Him two or three times throughout one day.

For us, getting in a good worship time is like getting in good food. Let me explain.

We all know about the food pyramid. There was a time when

I worried over my family's daily intake of food. I wanted to be sure each person received a daily portion of fruit, vegetables, protein and other things on the food pyramid. I felt like a failure if one of my children missed one of those health builders on a particular day.

A dear friend of mine, a school administrator, counseled me not to worry about balancing the intake of food on a daily basis. She said that it was better to look over the whole week and determine whether any adjustments were necessary in our diets.

It was good counsel, and I believe the same thing applies to our family's spiritual life. As families, we have lots to do. We need to work, carry out church responsibilities, buy groceries, do laundry, take baths, give baths, cook, clean the house and take out the garbage.

Worship Is Like Hugging or Kissing Your Children

Worship is different. Ideally, worship should spring from a loving relationship with God. It's like hugging or kissing your children. Is that particular act duty, or is it love? Worship should be like hugging or kissing your children. It should flow naturally out of a grateful, loving heart.

In my family, we don't have set rules that we must worship at specific times every day to show God we love Him or in order to stay close to Him. We need to abide in Him, not in our good works. True freedom is found in the family who simply loves God and spends their spare moments expressing it.

Jesus said that if we love Him, we will fulfill all the law. And if we love Him, praising Him will flow naturally throughout our week. If church day rolls around, and you realize you've been so caught up with the affairs of life all week that you haven't taken time to worship Him, then it's time to reprioritize. Make room for God. Ideally, we should be able to abide in Him and flow, allowing Him to lead us in all of our relationships and events.

The apostle Paul reminds us, "For as many as are led by the

Spirit of God, these are sons of God" (Rom. 8:14). The important thing is to stay vertically connected with our God, letting Him lead the way to highest household praise!

Music Is for Babies, Too!

Did you know that a newborn's brain is composed of nearly 100 billion brain cells? For the brain to work properly, those cells need to start communicating with each other. The more connections they make, the better.

Music, rhyme and intentional play help your child's mind develop. Studies have found that an infant recognizes and is soothed by the musical qualities in her mother's voice. This finding only confirms what mothers of many cultures have known for centuries—singing a lullaby brings a sense of security and sanctuary to their baby.

Speaking to your child may help in brain development, and a child under one year of age learns better when her parents speak to her in a high-pitched, singsong manner. Babies love repetitious rhythms and rhymes.

Now, with all that said, I'm glad that singing is good for their little brains, but we use music anyway just because it ministers to that other vital part of their being—their spirit!

An Available Basket of Instruments

When Johnathan was an infant, I decided to begin collecting children's instruments to store in a big round basket that sits beside the piano. I'm blessed to know how to play the piano. Countless times the little ones gather up instruments (always making sure Daddy has one, too), and Mom plays the piano while everyone else praises the Lord on the tambourines, maracas, drums, guitars, ukulele, bells and even baby rattles. We've used pots and pans with spoons plenty of times. We sing, jump, dance and play our instruments.

Just as often, one of them will put in a praise tape while Mom is busy cooking or cleaning. Joy and peace begin to flow into our home. Sometimes I'll stop what I'm doing and join them, scooping up a little one and twirling to the music.

For those of us interested in the psychiatric end of things, I will add this tidbit. Sally J. Rogers, Ph.D., assistant professor of psychiatry at the University of Colorado Health Sciences Center, reports that giving young children the chance to experience a variety of musical activities can assist them in learning language skills.[1] Now that's a great plus!

My journal is filled with preschool praise times we have spent together in our home. (What can I say? Some parents take pictures, some take home videos—I write words.) Let's take a peek.

Praise Journals

Morning praise

This week we praised and worshiped in the morning. Eleven-month-old Eden stood at the couch, patting her tambourine and maracas. Johnathan, three years old, played guitar, sang and danced with his sword, waved a white burp cloth and "ran for joy." I was at the piano. Over and over we sang, "God Didn't Give Me a Spirit of Fear."

Johnathan came over to the piano and said, "Mommy, I'm all wet."

I said, "Oh, good, Johnathan. That means you're like David. He danced so hard he took his shirt off."

"I'm like David," he shouted, taking off his flannel shirt and continuing to dance with all his being.

Dance praise

I was practicing (at the piano) for a tape I was planning to record. Fourteen-month-old Eden was running back and forth singing, "Ahhahhhahh." Then she'd stop and bend her knees and bounce a dance. She kept picking up the tambourine or maracas, shaking them while running or dancing or singing.

Her favorite thing is to come and play on the piano beside me. She stands there looking up at her fingers pressing keys and "Aahahahahhh" goes the song!

One night I turned on our children's church music tape as I began to clean up from supper. Baby Eden wasn't finished, so I was a bit perturbed when she demanded to get out of her high chair. I let her out, watching her closely. She sought out the source of the music, then danced and turned twirls in her baby way.

Love praise

Today Eden jumped and Johnathan danced to a *Manifest the Call* tape. Four-year-old Johnathan would dance and then come over and report to me what he was doing. "Mommy, I'm pointing my fingers up to God (while running in circles), and He's pointing down at me. We love each other, so that's why we're doing that!"

His little face is so expressive.

Joyful noise praise

Praise music is rocking the living room. Five-year-old Johnathan has a drum on the chair and a cymbal sitting on the antennas to his walkie-talkie, and he's playing away. Eden was playing her own drum and xylophone. Then she disappeared somewhere. Baby Judah was hitting the big plastic drum hung (safely) over her neck. Then she gave it up, and now she's hitting Johnathan's walkie-talkie cymbal. He's nice about it. Today it's Ron Kenoly's tape *Sing Out*.

PAJAMA PRAISE PARTY

There are nights when everyone seems to be dragging through the routine of eating snacks, brushing teeth, putting on pajamas and getting that last drink of water. Of course, every kid knows what's coming next—bedtime! Why is it that children dread the bed?

On the evenings when it's getting particularly difficult to inspire them onward, we declare a "pajama praise party."

The announcement goes something like this. "OK, if you all get on your pj's, eat your snack and brush your teeth really fast, we'll have a pajama praise party!"

The enthusiasm soars. All kids love a party, and this one is particularly goofy, with everyone hopping around in jammies. (It's good to make the last few songs the slow worshipful kind to help them maintain their peace for bedtime.)

They usually finish the bedtime routines in record time and still end up getting into bed at about the same time they would have with everyone dragging around.

As parents, our excitement (or lack of it) rubs off on our children. They can tell when we're excited to get into our pajamas and praise God. Our fiery zeal catches on with them, and off they go!

My husband and I try to work as a team. Sometimes my husband is tired from a long day's work, and I need to initiate the praise time. Other times I'm worn down from dealing with preschoolers all day, and he needs to step in and lead the show. That's the beauty of being married—the love and the teamwork between us.

If you're a single parent, get ready for a bedtime blast! Taking fifteen to thirty minutes to praise God takes the stress out of a day and shows children the "goofy" and relaxed side of Mom or Dad.

Where to Start

If worshiping God on your living room floor is a new concept to you, it may be difficult to know where to begin. Try buying three or four loud, noisy, obnoxious instruments. (Smile.) Keep them in a spot that's reachable and available to your child at any time.

Play tapes or CDs of praise music throughout your day or evening. Tapes are nice because older preschoolers can play them independently on their little Fisher Price tape recorders.

Pick up one of those instruments while you're walking through the living room. Bang on that noisy critter for just two minutes. Your child will love it!

Most importantly, learn how to have fun with your children while they're praising God. God expects children to be children—laughing, jumping and singing.

Go ahead—put on those jammies and twirl a toddler or two in the air. You'll get the "joy, joy, joy, joy down in your heart to stay!"

IN CLOSING...

Can you feel God's excitement about praise in your house? He smiles with pleasure at the chubby little hands that are raised in sheer joy on your living room floor.

> I will sing of the mercies of the LORD forever;
> With my mouth will I make known
> Your faithfulness to all generations.
>
> —PSALM 89:1

Father God, in Jesus' name I pray...

Does your preschooler love to sing or dance? Does he seem to gravitate to a particular instrument or style of praise? Write some of your observations here.

What steps can you take to incorporate new styles of "preschool praise" into your home?

Winning the No-No War

5

About two months before giving birth to my second child, my twenty-two-month-old son, Johnathan, displayed his worst side.

He declared his independence through a war of wills. His reply for every direction given was an emphatic *no*.

He screamed and cried when I changed his diaper or fed him his breakfast. He had a long list of answers:

"I don't *want* to pray."

"I don't *want* to go nighty-night."

"I don't *want* cereal."

Once he took off running in a crowded department store. It was a mother's nightmare. Of course, I lumbered after him, eight months pregnant and in a panic to find my toddler. It took awhile, and you can guess what he said when I found him at a checkout counter about six aisles over.

"I don't *want* to go."

At church services, I would cringe when I saw the children's church director coming into the adult church service to get either my husband or me. Johnathan often decided he didn't *want* to go to his toddler class and howled loud and long enough to voice his opinion to several other classes.

Bedtime Battles

Bedtime was the worst. He refused to be laid down. He screamed, jumped up and down in his bed and threw himself down. One night, I walked away from his crib while he was screaming at me, "I don't *want* to go nighty-night!"

"I know, Honey," I softly replied. "But it's time to go nighty-night, and Mommy wants you to go to sleep."

I left the room, leaving the door partly open as usual, and he started his normal tantrum. Suddenly, I heard a thump, and I ran into the bedroom. There he was on the floor, half-crying because he had hurt himself and half-triumphant because he was out of that crib!

"I don't want to go nighty-night," he insisted.

He was in tears, and I was in tears, too. I knew he really could have hurt himself, and I was honestly at a loss as to what to do. I called my pediatrician. He advised that I shut the bedroom door and let him scream it out.

I was desperate enough to try it. The first night I called a girlfriend while Johnathan was throwing a fit in his bedroom with the door shut. She couldn't believe the doctor told me to do that. Again, I cried. (A parent who's been through this frustration knows how it can bring you to tears.)

After I got off the phone, Johnathan flipped himself out of his crib again. The doctor had told me not to go in the room. I delayed until I noticed a change in his crying. Then I flew into the room to find him standing on the floor with a cut lip, still demanding to get his own way. I sat on the floor and cried, rocking him and praying again for answers.

REBELLION OR INDIVIDUALITY?

Looking back, I can only wish that I had enjoyed the benefit of the teaching ministry of John and Paula Sandford of Elijah House Ministry when Johnathan was going through his no-no phase.[1] According to the Sandfords, the first stage of basic emotional trust transitions into the second stage of individuation where the two- to four-year-old child learns to distinguish himself from his parent and discovers, "I am not an extension of you."

As the child realizes that he is his own person, he will venture to say *no* even to the parent he depends upon for his survival. He learns that if he runs from Mommy, he will be chased. The "upside" of this new discovery is that there is a new ability to also be intimate with the parent, to show love from this "new person" he is becoming.

The Sandfords encourage parents to foster their child's individuality and try to avoid control issues as much as possible. An Elijah House teacher, Linda Forster, suggests initiating a "control bank" where the parent sets up situations where the child can deposit making some of his own decisions.

For example, let him choose whether he wants to put on his jammies or brush his teeth first. It doesn't really matter which one is first, as long as both get done!

When Eden was a toddler (and even a baby), I held up three dresses in front of her just to see which one she would gravitate toward. Invariably, she always chose a royal blue or navy blue dress over every other color in front of her. Allowing your child to make certain small decisions like this can help him feel like he is more in control of his world and able to be his own person. (It can also give the parents some early hints as to what their child may enjoy or be good at later on in life.)

After these "deposits" are made into your child's control bank, Linda says that the parent can make a "withdrawal" out of the bank without depleting his independence. For example, if you tell your child you need to leave and he refuses to budge, you can pick him up and carry him to the car without crushing his individuality.

The idea here is to work with the child's need for control instead of butting heads against him!

We didn't have this wonderful "control bank" teaching to lean on, but I do remember giving Johnathan some choices about which vegetable, snack or shoes he wanted to wear. Looking back, I wish we had given him more choices. Wisdom tends to grow with the years, and we gave our second and third child more choices during these crucial years.

I ask God for wisdom to help us discern if the root cause for our child's no-no is outright defiance (rebellion) or whether he is simply reaching for the important emotional step of independence.

It's difficult to judge, but we are not alone. As we ask God for wisdom, He can give us wisdom to know the difference. And we can continue to make at least one or two deposits daily into our child's control bank, allowing him to make simple decisions during his daily routines and experiences.

I believe that God can help the parent sense when his child has gone past his need for individuality and into rebellion. While I believe in allowing a child to express his individuality, I think that we can go overboard in letting him run the entire show every day. I know some women (grandmothers are particularly keen at this) who gear their entire day around what the child wants. The truth is there is no end to "I want"; it is a bottomless bucket. Self-control over "I want" starts when a child first reaches his hand out to turn the knobs on the stove or dishwasher. And even though our child doesn't know it, boundaries in his life are there to keep him from getting hurt.

God knows the hearts of children. God didn't tell us to squash our children's curiosity, but to raise them and nurture them, helping them to grow according to their particular "bend" in life. Somewhere during the years of two to four, your child will want to launch into discovering who he is and how he fits into the world around him. Part of the job of parenting is to find out the "why" of our child's behavior and respond to him accordingly.

PADDLE IN FAITH THAT THE WORD WORKS

Now, let me return to our story about Johnathan's no-no war. The days turned into weeks and the weeks into months, and Johnathan's behavior improved little. By now you're probably thinking, *Did you try paddling him?* We did.

> Foolishness is bound up in the heart of a child; the rod of correction will drive it far from him.
>
> —PROVERBS 22:15

> The devising of foolishness is sin.
>
> —PROVERBS 24:9

A *fool* can be described as someone who acts irresponsibly—like not wanting to sleep at night. The opposite of being irresponsible is to be responsible or accountable for our actions. Granted, he was only two years old. But even a two-year-old can grasp the fact that our bodies must go to bed every night to rest.

Paddling is not the first discipline we resort to with our little ones, but in the war of the wills, it wins. Before we paddled, we usually talked to him about his behavior and then prayed, "Lord, we are paddling our son in faith that the rod will do what Your Word says it will do."

We didn't beat him. We didn't pat him. We administered one to three swats with a wooden spoon onto his diaper.

> He who spares his rod hates his son, but he who loves him disciplines him promptly.
>
> —Proverbs 13:24

We often quoted these scriptures before a paddling, believing that they would produce the effect promised in the Word of God. Johnathan seemingly did not respond to most paddlings. The truth is, he didn't seem to respond to anything we tried. He continued to rebel at every direction. We decided to meet his rebellion with faith in the Word. We didn't spank him for every little thing, only for outright defiance—the "no, no" thing. And each time he decided to buck what we told him to do, we spoke the Scriptures over him and spanked him and hugged him. I remember crying more than he did.

> Now no chastening [discipline] seems to be joyful for the present, but painful; nevertheless, afterward it yields the peaceable fruit of righteousness to those who have been trained by it.
>
> —Hebrews 12:11

Fruit usually takes a long time to grow. We had to be patient.

The Fruitful Season

After several months of consistent love and discipline, we finally won the no-no war. Johnathan began to respond to our directions without temper tantrums. He knew Mom and Dad wouldn't give up or give in until he obeyed.

Six months after the bedtime battles, when he was two and one-half years old, Johnathan came out of his room with the paddle in his hand. It was time to read stories before bed, but he began to rehearse his don't do list.

"Don't do...or you'll get paddled. You got to obey. Don't do ... no, no."

Then he toddled over in front of me.

"Mommy, I lay hands on the paddle. Mommy, lay your hand on the paddle."

I looked at him like, "Why?" but I did it.

"I pray," he explained in his simple way.

This time I obeyed Johnathan.

"Jesus," he started. "I thank You for this paddle. Help to obey. And it drives out rebellion (wee-bellion). In Jesus' name, amen."

Praise God. He was catching on!

THE "MEAN" PARENT

For paddling to produce the best results, both mother and father need to agree upon its use. In some families, grandparents or aunts or uncles may not approve of paddling, and this can produce added tension in the early stages of discipline. It's doubly difficult if the preschooler's parents are not in full agreement.

Whatever methods you use to discipline your child, it's imperative that you respond to his disobedience as a team. Parents should try to reach a point of agreement in discipline, even if it means some compromise on the part of one or both of you. Your children will feel more secure when both parents agree to discipline in the same way with unity and teamwork.

When I say "discipline in the same way," I don't mean that both parents correct children the same way for every little squabble. That's almost impossible. Each parent brings a different quality into the mix of discipline. For example, while I make the children sit on the couch, Scott may tell them to go to their rooms for a few minutes. But when you're facing the no-no war, you need unity, or the discipline itself can become a major point of contention between the parents. It's better to agree upon a method of discipline before the next no-no war breaks out.

Single parents face the most difficult dilemma—if the child is allowed to throw tantrums at Mommy's house but is stopped when she tries that with Daddy, she may say hurtful things to her father such as, "You're mean. I want to stay with Mommy."

If that's your situation, your best reaction is to remain unruffled emotionally. Don't allow those kinds of statements to strike fear or alarm in your heart, or your child will then have a method of controlling you through that fear. Your response to your child must remain consistent. God has given you His grace to parent your child. She needs boundaries, and she needs you to show her what is right and wrong behavior.

Although you shouldn't belittle the absent parent, you can say, "I am your father (or mother), and you must obey me." Later on, when your child is quietly playing and not currently being corrected for something, you can take three minutes to explain to her that you love her and don't want her to get hurt, and that's why she has to listen to what you say.

One young adult daughter of divorced parents told me that it was confusing to her to see two different worlds as a child. Her father was a strict but loving disciplinarian who took her to church and spent time with her. Her mother was just "around" and never took her to church, but let her do whatever she wanted. She said that, as a child, she naturally played into what she thought was fun—having her own way. But as she grew older, she could see that the loving disciplinarian parent showed the most love toward her, and she is now striving to be that kind of parent to her own daughter.

Remember that your preschooler needs you to show her what is right. She needs you to stop her when she is demanding her way. Deep inside, children want someone to discipline and protect them with boundaries. That is the very heart of love. Sin hurts, and sin will hurt your children if you do not step in to stop the wrong patterns of behavior and show them the right ways to handle themselves.

SIN HURTS

A word about paddling. Some Christian leaders recommend using a hand when paddling in order to avoid abusive spanking. I have heard others say that if the parent uses his hand, he confuses the child because the hand is what fed him and held him and shouldn't be seen as an object of discipline. Others say that the hand is the perfect tool for spanking for the same reason!

Theories on discipline, especially spanking, have been introduced and reintroduced for centuries. It is no wonder some of us feel unsure of ourselves when disciplining our children. When I am unsure of what to do, I turn to prayer and to the Word.

I want to reiterate what the Bible says. The Bible says to use a rod, not a whip or a belt.

If we choose to use the rod, we must remember that the rod is a discipline device, not a weapon, so we sometimes have our children sit on the couch if we are upset. Then later, when we are no longer frustrated or upset, we instruct and discipline as needed.

When we paddle our children, we tell them, "Sin hurts. Your sin is hurting you, and the Bible says that this paddle will drive out the sin." I even encourage my children to picture their sin being "driven" out the window of the house. I've often said, "Look, that lie just flew right out the window!"

Children may respond differently when corrected. One may become angry when told *no* or paddled. Another may cry and need to say "I'm sorry" before the discipline is effective. There are those precious few who cry the first time you say *no* and immediately change their bad behavior.

Paddling the little one isn't an end in itself. In fact, we reserve the paddle for outright defiance that we sense is rooted in rebellion. For example, if a child didn't clean up right away when he was told, or he hit his sister, we wouldn't spank him for that. But if he openly defies one of us and declares *no* to a direction given, we see that as rebellion, and the little one receives a rod to drive this root of rebellion far from him and far from our home.

Besides, rebellion can be contagious—brothers and sisters may "catch it" if it is not stopped right away!

Showing Bible verses as our authority in right and wrong, we should instruct our children in what is and isn't acceptable behavior in God's eyes. (And then throw them on the floor and tickle them until they scream!)

Correct Immediately

Did you notice the last word in Proverbs 13:24? It says that the parent who loves his child will discipline him "promptly."

On particularly crazy days it's tempting for Mom to tell a willful child, "I'll tell Daddy when he gets home, and he'll deal with you." Do you know that most dads really don't appreciate that plan?

A small child needs to be corrected immediately because most often, within an hour he will forget what he did right or wrong. When there's a time lapse between the offense and the correction, the correction given seems unfair at best and often confusing.

Besides, sin left uncorrected will lead to more sin. Sin begets sin! In the hour(s) you wait to handle the problem, the problem will get bigger. It's like putting out a fire. You need to stop it before it mounts to a huge blaze.

Small children need an immediate response to their sinful behavior.

With each child, we need to do all we know to do and then stand in faith that the Word works.

Let me repeat that. *The Word works.*

Can Spanking Harm My Child?

As parents, my husband and I rely on Scripture and our personal convictions before God. However, I also want to relate a study that was conducted in 2001 and presented at a meeting of the American Psychological Association. Although psychologists are often the first to tell us we shouldn't spank our children, this study found that "mild to moderate spanking did not have any negative social or emotional effects on children when compared to children who were not spanked at all."

A researcher in the study, Diana Baumrind, said, "It is reliance on physical punishment [alone], not whether or not it is used at all, that is associated with harm to the child." Only a small minority of parents ever reached this level of punishment, the researchers said.[2]

Because spanking is viewed by some people as abusive, I feel it is wise to administer paddling within the confines of the home. Outsiders have been known to report parents, even good Christian parents, for spanking outside the confines of their home. If we prepare our children for where they are going and what is expected from them before they arrive at a store, church or to see relatives, we can often avoid temper tantrums and clashes in public places. However, if a spanking is necessary, the laws are behind the parent, not the outsider.

PERSONAL VIEWPOINTS

When you read chapter fifteen, "Prepared for Service," you will understand why I would not want to give a public school system or public family day care permission to spank my child. My own childhood experience with corporal punishment in the public school system years ago was a living nightmare. Frankly, I'm glad that most public school systems do not allow teachers to spank children.

It is possible, however, to find a Christian school that upholds your values and discipline patterns at home. There are a few precious Christian day-care centers or Christian schools where a parent may feel comfortable giving a Christian teacher permission to spank his or her child in certain circumstances.

Interestingly, when I worked as a day-care teacher, I had one two-year-old who flew in the door like lightning. As the day wore on, the little tyke liked to hit other children, tear down their play area and display anger at being told what to do. His father and mother were Christians, and they honestly begged me to spank him for his unruly behavior. The day care I was in forbid spanking by the staff or teachers, so the father gave me his work phone number and requested that I call him if his son grew far out of hand. Throughout the school year, I called the father only two times. The toddler caught onto the fact that his actions in the school were going to be met with Dad, and he learned to change his behavior.

Spanking and Foster Care

I would like to quickly delve into a few parental viewpoints concerning spanking in foster care.

Foster care is an entirely different discipline matter. I've heard Christian parents complain about the banning of corporal punishment with foster children. Some have even said that if they're not allowed to spank, then they won't take in foster children because it ruins the authority and disciplinary guidelines already established in their home.

While it's true that raising a house full of children with two separate standards may be a bit challenging, I think that the welfare of the foster child is paramount. A child who has been abused, beaten or even normally "spanked" with anger (hitting a child with anger is not a biblically based spanking) will not be able to receive a loving spanking from a foster parent in the same way as that parent's own child can. Most children in foster care have special emotional issues that must be handled with sacrificial, unconditional love and loyalty regardless of the child's actions.

One couple walked into the office of their foster child's caseworker, observing his walls decorated with many framed certificates and credentials for his service to children. The caseworker asked the couple during the interview how they planned to discipline their new foster child.

This couple said that although they did spank their own children, they would not spank her because she was not brought up under the same conditions as their biological children. They had agreed before walking into the office that they would find other methods of disciplining, such as sending her to her room or taking away privileges.

Imagine their surprise when the caseworker responded to their spanking viewpoints with, "That's awesome! Can I write that down?"

This man and wife worked in an inner-city ministry, and they took in many children. In fact, there wasn't a child they wouldn't take in. Children in wheelchairs, with walkers and with high needs were placed in their loving care. May I tell you a couple of their stories?

Two preschool brothers were brought into their home. The youngest was in diapers, and the older one was soon discovered to have a fixation with the vacuum cleaner. He would stand outside the closet door and beg to have it brought out. As soon as the vacuum cleaner was within reach, the older boy hugged it for all he was worth, and his little brother followed his example.

The boys' caseworker said that this had been an ongoing behavior pattern. The caseworker just allowed the boys to hug the vacuum cleaner. The foster mother often pulled the boys to herself and hugged them with a mother's love. (A child psychologist can analyze this one; I just want to tell you the story.) The important thing here is that these boys, even if for a short time, received love and acceptance modeled by a loving married couple.

Another little baby came through the doors of this home. This sweet little fifteen-month-old baby had curly blond hair and blue eyes and was already potty trained. She arrived at this couple's home literally exhausted. Her tiny face had bruises, telltale signs of abuse at home. Abigail had few clothes and even fewer smiles. She never cried out in her sleep, but clung to open arms whenever they were offered to her. Abigail was only there for a few weeks, but during those days she was loved.

This couple took in many teen girls who had been abused as well. Let me tell you the results of this foster home in the mother's own words:

> Each child who passed through our home was unique and special. Some stayed for one night, some for months. One stayed for two years. She was a daughter to us and a sister to our own biological children. When she left, it broke our hearts.

Still, this foster mother experienced the reward of being a mother to many! She told me:

> One day in a grocery store I heard, "Mom... Mom!" I didn't recognize the voice, so I kept going. Soon I was in the embrace of a young lady who knew me personally. She had indeed been one of our many houseguests. Some of the girls still stay in touch. While some are doing well, others are not. But God placed them with us for a season, and we have to trust that even though they're moving on with their lives, they're taking with them some of the things we tried to instill in them.

A Prayer From the Past

Preschool parenting isn't always easy. Amid the daily sacrifices of giving beyond what we thought we would ever be able to give, there are times we blow it and need to run to God for forgiveness and help. I would like to end this chapter with a prayer that George Washington recorded in his prayer diary, *Daily Sacrifice:*

> O God, who art rich in mercy and plenteous in redemption, mark not, I beseech Thee, what I have done amiss; remember that I am but dust, and remit my transgressions, negligences and ignorances, and cover them all with the absolute obedience of Thy dear Son...[3]

It's a good prayer—for mothers and fathers of preschoolers and even the father of our nation. Not one of us does everything right, but God is right there to dust us off, forgive us and give us strength to try again.

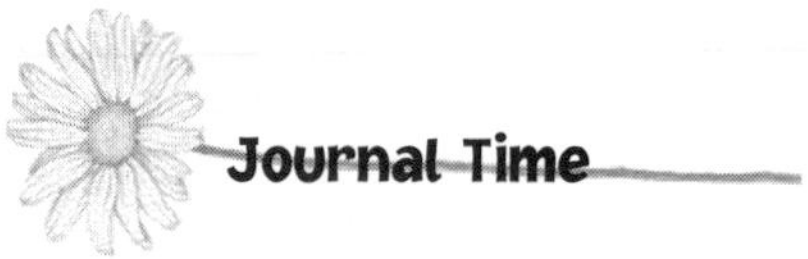

Journal Time

> My son, do not despise the chastening of the LORD,
> Nor detest His correction;
> For whom the LORD loves He corrects,
> Just as a father the son in whom he delights.
>
> —PROVERBS 3:11–12

Father God, in Jesus' name I pray…

Has reading this chapter encouraged your heart that you have been doing something right? Or perhaps you are relieved that you are not alone in your ventures to discipline according to the Bible. Why not take a moment to jot down a few things that you feel you are doing right in the area of discipline?

Are there any changes you would like to make in the methods you use to discipline your child?

The Law Is a Teacher 6

Five-year-old Johnathan came home from school one Wednesday, stirred with excitement about chapel. (Chapel is a Christian school term for a student assembly where everyone meets with God.) He told his three-year-old sister, Eden, "Chapel was so much fun today. We did all kinds of neat stuff." Then he went into his "teaching mode."

"Eden, when you go to school, you'll have to go to chapel. Chapel's where you sing some songs and then listen to the teacher talk."

"Nuh-uh," answered Eden, in her know-it-all tone of voice. "You don't listen to the teacher; you listen to God and the Holy Spirit."

Johnathan thought about that for a moment. "Well, you listen to them a little bit, but mostly you listen to the teacher."

Isn't that a hoot? They're both right.

Trained to Hear the Holy Spirit

Until the time that our children are born again and learn to know the voice and presence of the Holy Spirit consistently, we will be the words of Jesus to which they listen and the Bible that they read.

And before we even ask Him, God is interested in leading our little families.

> He shall feed his flock like a shepherd: he shall gather the lambs with his arm, and carry them in his bosom, and shall gently lead those that are with young.
>
> —Isaiah 40:11, KJV

Notice that God states He leads the whole flock. But He holds the lambs and gently leads those that are with young—that's us!

He is infinitely more interested in leading our young family than we can imagine.

Little lambs are trained to hear the voice of the shepherd, too. Even an infant will turn its head toward its mother whenever she speaks. God tells us that we turn our head when He speaks, too.

In John 10, Jesus says that He knows His sheep and calls them out by name. His sheep hear His voice, and they follow Him.

Romans 8:14 says, "Those who are led by the Spirit of God are sons of God" (NIV).

Interestingly, Galatians 5:18 says, "If you are led by the Spirit, you are not under law." Precisely! The law is a tutor to bring us to Christ so that we are no longer led by the "dos" and "don'ts" but by the wonderful Holy Spirit of God!

> But the Helper, the Holy Spirit, whom the Father will send in My name, He will teach you all things, and bring to your remembrance all things that I said to you.
>
> —JOHN 14:26

One of our biggest goals in raising our preschoolers is to help them hear the Holy Spirit so that we can stop talking! That may sound silly, but our future plan is to back off gradually from giving directions. Our hope is to watch our children enter their teen years listening more keenly and obediently to the Holy Spirit's voice. John 14:26 says that the Holy Spirit will bring to their remembrance what we have taught them and what the Bible says. I fully trust the Holy Spirit to do His job!

That doesn't mean that preschoolers don't hear the voice of God. Chapter sixteen goes into some detail on how many children hear God in timely and beautiful ways. Still, children need the help of the Bible and boundaries set by their parents in order to mature in their walk in the Spirit. For now, Daddy and Mommy provide a large part of God's Word and God's face. (Makes me want to write that chapter on images all over again.)

Teach the Rules

Here's what God expects from parents:

> And these words which I command you today shall be in your heart; you shall teach them diligently to your children, and shall talk of them when you sit in your house, when you walk by the way, when you lie down, and when you rise up.
>
> —Deuteronomy 6:6–7

Godly parenting must begin with rules—God's rules, government rules, household rules, church rules and school rules. Rules bring boundaries into our children's lives and provide safety and security to grow in Christ. That doesn't mean we hit them over the head with rules! Let it flow naturally in the course of the day. Home is a wonderful place to learn and grow!

The very heart of Christian parenting is to lead a child to be a disciple of Jesus Christ. It's a joy to a parent's heart to hear a child praying in bed after lights-out or singing a song from his heart while riding in his car seat in the back seat of the car. It's incredible when you watch children sharing a favorite toy instead of arguing over it.

But what does it take to bring a child to the point of singing or praying to God in private? What makes a three-year-old finally decide to share a toy instead of screaming, "It's mine?"

It takes a lot of defining boundaries and establishing rules. It takes a lot of teaching and patience. Boundaries do not just fall from heaven and hit children on the head. They fall from our mouths and our countenances, forming a safe, peaceful framework in which our children can freely grow.

Peaceable Fruit of Righteousness

Just look at the fruit of a child whose early training begins with the "law" (or God's rules):

> But after faith has come, we are no longer under a tutor.
>
> —Galatians 3:25

Right now, we're the teacher or tutor with the law book (God's Word) in our hands. But when faith comes into your child's heart, you will be able to trust him, step by step, to do what is right without having to command him from God's rules. This type of parenting brings that peaceful fruit of righteousness, and the Father is glorified.

> No chastening [discipline] seems to be joyful for the present, but painful; nevertheless, afterward it yields the peaceable fruit of righteousness to those who have been trained by it.
>
> —HEBREWS 12:11

Notice the word *peaceable*. Sin brings confusion, strife and disorder. The truth is, sin hurts. Don't be afraid to say "Sin hurts" aloud to your child.

The parent who is willing to discipline and instruct her child is able to enjoy (periodic) fruits of peace in their home.

We go in cycles around our home. It seems we have a week or so of continuous training, disciplining and teaching our children on a particular behavior, and then we'll experience a period of peace in that area. Then we'll find we're in another phase of training, followed by yet another interlude of peace. Praise God, His Word works!

EARLY BIBLE FOUNDATIONS

When I was an infant, my parents had been saved only four years and attended a Baptist church. My dad looked forward to coming home each night from work to find me "waiting up" for him. Night after night he picked me up and quoted scriptures in my ear. No one taught him to do that; he just did it. By the time I was three, I could quote the Twenty-third Psalm as well as many other verses.

My mother read to my brother and me from devotional books and Bible storybooks. I still remember the location of the chair we sat in together as she read to us. We were in church every time the door swung open.

Shortly after salvation, at four years of age, I had a tremendous turmoil of soul. I wanted to know exactly what God required of me. My mom read to me from Kenneth Taylor's book *The Bible in Pictures for Little Eyes*.[1]

My favorite story was Abraham and Isaac. In fact, I called the book, "Man's Lovin' Book," which I named after Abraham's great love for his son and his God. I remember my great love for that story, and I'm told I asked to read it almost on a daily basis. My parents didn't know what treasures God was pouring into me from that story, but the Holy Spirit was moving mightily! When my mother opened up that story and read it to me, I was hearing God speak to my heart.

Clearly I remember my dad standing in the doorway to the kitchen when I cornered him and asked him, "Daddy, will you put me on the altar like Isaac?"

"God's not going to ask me to do that," he answered.

"Yeah, but if He did, would you do it, Daddy?" I asked again.

Dad laughed, "God's not going to ask me to do that, Sis."

"Yeah, but what if He did tell you to do it, would you?" I insisted. I had to have an answer to that question. There was no peace in me until it was settled. I had to know if my dad would obey God as Isaac's dad did.

I persisted, "Would you do it? If God told you to do it, would you?"

Seeing that I wasn't going to let him off the hook, he finally gave me his answer. I held my breath.

"If God told me to do that, which He isn't going to..."

"Daddy!"

"If God told me to sacrifice you on the altar, I would obey God. But He's not going to tell me that."

I ignored his last statement and distinctly decided, "Then I'm willing to be like Isaac. I'm willing to go the altar if God tells me to."

I believe at that exact moment, I had fully dedicated my life to the Lord Jesus, ready to die for His name. And I knew exactly what I was doing. It may seem radical to others, but when my father told me he would obey God like Abraham, I felt more secure than ever before in my life. I needed to know that, above all else, no matter what, my dad would obey God.

TEACHING BIBLE VERSES

I'm sharing so many stories to implant the thought that God's Holy Spirit truly does speak to children through verses and Bible stories.

I'm not doing as well as my dad did with me in teaching my children to quote Scripture. At least, I'm not using the same methods.

I have taught them some verses by repetition as we have needed it, but honestly, they learn many scriptures through Steve Green's scriptures-in-song video, *Hide 'Em in Your Heart*. (Mom and Dad are learning a few more scriptures, too.)

My friend has her children march around the living room holding up picture posters that show what the verse means. After a few laps around the living room, the verse is still "marching" in their hearts. The key here is to have fun and relax.

Your local Christian bookstore should be able to direct you to several great DVDs and CDs now available. The DVDs are fun to watch, and singing the songs in the car makes Scripture memorization easier than ever.

If you want your child to memorize a particular verse that isn't on a DVD or CD, you may want to put it to music yourself. Just for fun, here's John 3:16 to the tune of "Mary Had a Little Lamb."

> God so loved the world He gave, world He gave, world
> He gave,
> God so loved the world He gave His only begotten Son.

My children particularly enjoy the rhythm and rhyme of rap. Ephesians 6:10 is a great verse, which we turned into a "rap" sound. Children don't really sing this verse, but they clap or beat it out on pots and pans. The asterisk * sign means to clap or beat an "instrument" at that part. Here we go! (Say the words fast. It's even more fun if you sway back and forth as you clap it out.)

> BE strong * *
> In the LORD * *
> And the power * *
> Of His MIGHT!
> (Now punch into the air and yell, "PUNCH IT OUT!" and repeat the rap.)

Want to have more fun with this? OK, try dressing up your child in a cool (or crazy) hat and sunglasses. Now, PUNCH IT OUT! Yep, time to get out the video camera.

Now, imagine forwarding that video camera fifteen years to when your child is in high school facing a gym or art class where the requirements seem beyond his skill level. Mom and Dad are not around, but because you have "downloaded" this verse into his little heart, the Holy Spirit can now bring it back to his memory to bring him faith for God's power and strength just when he needs it.

Baby's Secure Foundations

From infancy to about two years of age, we taught our children that God made the world, God made them, they are special, and Jesus loves them. We used all the visuals and action songs we could find. We turned on peaceful, joyous Christian music.

Spiritually speaking, infants need to know that their home is secure, at peace and that their needs will be met. The church nursery needs to tingle with that same atmosphere. Your baby should feel peace, protection, care and love in the house of God. Baby's first impressions of the house of God are important!

Sometime after two years of age, we began to teach our children God's rules.

THE TEN RULES

Praise God for the Ten Commandments! Listening to the story of Moses receiving the ten rules from God ministers to children.

Eden was two and one-half years old before she would sit still long enough for me to read the short story of the Ten Commandments. For days after that first breakthrough, she pulled out her little picture Bible on her own and looked up the story. Her sleep even improved.

Now it's Eden's favorite story, and we have read it together over and over again.

We like to read from Kenneth Taylor's book *My First Bible in Pictures*.[2] My children and I turn to the page where Moses is standing with the stones in his hands on Mount Sinai. I have them hold out their little hands, and I touch each finger, counting, "1, 2, 3, 4, 5, 6, 7, 8, 9, 10."

Then I hold out both of my hands and, with gusto, announce, "Ten rules! God says obey the ten rules. One rule says we only worship God. Another rule says always obey your mom and dad." (Presenting two rules is a good start for a preschooler.)

Then we turn the page. It's the one where the people are praying to the golden calf.

"OH, NO!" I exclaim. "What are the people doing?"

"NO, NO, NO!"

Their little eyes go wide, and they point and say, "No, no, no!" (I knew those no-nos would come in handy.) Little children are very happy to point out a no-no that someone else is doing.

I like to use the same tone of voice that I use when I see one of them tearing all the tissues out of the tissue box. I shake my finger at the people worshiping the idol and say, "No, no, you don't pray to idols."

OK, that's simple enough. But the gem here is that *no-no* is now connected with God and His Word. And in a delightful way, my child and I are now in full agreement concerning sin.

You know, while they're learning, you are having fun, too! I love to hear their words explaining what they're learning.

For example, when I was teaching them about Moses, I used large flashcards and explained how the Hebrews followed the cloud to the beautiful oasis called *Elim* where God told the people to pitch their tents and rest.

The look on my five-year-old's face told me that he didn't understand. So I explained again (and again).

I said, "The people were tired, so God told them to pitch their tents at this beautiful place and take a rest."

Finally Johnathan voiced his question, "Mom, why'd they throw all their tents away?"

Another time, he anxiously wanted to know whether or not his daddy could get a day off from work to go with him on an upcoming field trip.

It seemed that he thought Daddy worked as a slave in Egypt; he asked, "Daddy, did you ask your ruler yet if you could get off work, and did he let you?"

A Child Desires to Please His Parents

Even though their innocent perspectives make us howl sometimes, we have to face it: Children are born with a sin nature. They are naturally drawn to sin.

> Surely I was sinful at birth, sinful from the time my mother conceived me.
>
> —Psalm 51:5, NIV

However, one thing we have going for us as parents is that our children naturally desire to please us.

It's true. A child's desire to please his parents is a precious possession. This desire can be tarnished if a parent vents anger against the child or frustrates him by expecting more of him than is reasonable.

The Bible says, "And you, fathers, do not provoke your children to wrath, but bring them up in the training and admonition of the Lord" (Eph. 6:4). The child who desires to please his parent will submit to the loving discipline and consistent training given by the parent.

A WORD ABOUT DEPARTMENT STORES

Most parents have been through the embarrassment of hauling a screaming child out of a department or grocery store. I know I have. May I make a suggestion?

Leaders of trips to the department store need to let the followers know where they're going and what's expected of them. Believe it or not, we talk to our children about where we are going and what we are doing even when they are babies. I remember dropping off Johnathan at a close friend's house when he was only twenty-two months old and telling him exactly where we were going and when we would back. My friend laughed at how he looked at us right in the eyes as though he understood every word. He probably did!

Generally, children respond much better when they are told where they are going and what is expected of them versus being jolted from one place to the next without explanation. I try to tell my children on the way to the store why we're going and how I expect them to behave. When they're smaller, it benefits to promise good shoppers some play time with Daddy or even a quarter to get a (safe) prize out of the gumball machines as you leave the store.

I like to reward good behavior. Best of all, your child will, in time, develop the habit of being content while you're shopping.

THE FEAR OF THE LORD

"Laying down the law" often feels much more like police work than parenting. It would be a lot more convenient if we could just suggest and direct rather than command and expect. But our children's salvation actually depends upon our consistency in commanding them to obey. "Therefore the law was our tutor to bring us to Christ, that we might be justified by faith" (Gal. 3:24).

While working on this chapter, I've been using large flash cards to teach the life of Moses (again) to Johnathan and Eden (who are now five and three.) This morning they begged to hear the next story. So I told them the part about Mount Sinai when God spoke to the people through a cloud with thundering, lightning and a trumpet blast—it was quite a visual, audio lesson.

They were both impressed by God's awesome power. Respecting God's power, holiness and love is called "the fear of the Lord." To fear the Lord also means that we love what He loves and hate what He hates.

Children need the fear of the Lord in order to submit to correction and training.

> The fear of the LORD is the beginning of wisdom, and the knowledge of the Holy One is understanding.
>
> —PROVERBS 9:10

"THANK YOU FOR PADDLING ME"

One evening Johnathan and Eden got into a heated argument over who owned a pie fork. Their dad told them not to argue, but they got angrier and louder, ignoring his correction. Pretty soon, the family dinner table was at war. So Dad took them to our bedroom and told them that arguing with one another is not showing the fruit of love or self-control.

After a lengthy instruction and a short paddling, they both walked out of the bedroom teary-eyed, but at peace. Johnathan shocked us when he walked up to his father and said, "It's funny. I feel like I ought to thank you for paddling me."

I was sure I didn't hear that right. (I honestly didn't tell him I was writing a chapter on discipline.)

Daddy told him, "That's good, Johnathan. You should want to thank us, because the Bible says that the parent who loves his child will paddle him when he needs it. I paddled you because I love you."

So Johnathan thanked his dad for paddling him.

REASONABLE RULES AND WINNING WARS

This verse bears repeating here.

> No discipline seems pleasant at the time, but painful. Later on, however, it produces a harvest of righteousness and peace for those who have been trained by it.
>
> —HEBREWS 12:11, NIV

When I use the word *discipline,* I do not automatically refer to paddling a child for negative behavior. In fact, paddling is a last resort or reserved for the most severe trespasses. In our house, lying is a severe trespass and ends in an automatic paddling. (And because of this, lying is a rare occurrence.)

Discipline means training. It means (and this is the hard part) consistency. Discipline is not something that is done twice a day like brushing teeth. Instruction and discipline are a lifestyle. When a reasonable rule is established, the parent must not back down or give in. Neither can we allow the child to argue with our decision to discipline him or challenge our authority in any way.

DON'T JUST CORRECT, INSTRUCT!

Sometimes I miss it on the instruction end of things. I'll stop what I'm doing, "win the war" so to speak, warn them, administer a paddling or have them sit or whatever, and then I'm back to what I was doing before it all broke out.

My husband, Scott, is very big on instruction. For instance, in the pie fork dispute, he took both offenders into the bedroom and instructed both of them for at least ten minutes on the fruit of the Spirit. Once they both fully understood, he paddled them, and they received it with submissive hearts.

Here are some scriptures to strengthen those of us who prefer to busily bypass the instruction part of training.

> When I was my father's son, tender and the only one in the sight of my mother, he also taught me, and said to me: "Let your heart retain my words; keep my commands and live.

> Get wisdom! Get understanding! Do not forget, nor turn away from the words of my mouth."
>
> —Proverbs 4:3–5

> And these words which I command you today shall be in your heart. You shall teach them diligently to your children, and shall talk of them when you sit in your house, when you walk by the way, when you lie down, and when you rise up.
>
> —Deuteronomy 6:6–7

> All scripture is given by inspiration of God, and is profitable for doctrine, for reproof, for correction, for instruction in righteousness.
>
> —2 Timothy 3:16

I began this chapter with a story about Johnathan explaining to his little sister that she will need to listen to the teacher in chapel. Here's Johnathan's version of what he heard in chapel about the crippled man who was healed at the Gate Beautiful.

Jesus Healed the "Wrinkled" Man

I picked Johnathan up from school one Wednesday, and he was very expressive in telling me the story he learned in chapel that day.

"We learned about this really old man who was all wrinkled up," said Johnathan, squishing up his face to show me all the wrinkles.

"All wrinkled up?" I asked.

"Yeah, he was sitting at a gate, a real beautiful gate. The man was all wrinkled up, and he always walked like this," he explained, hunching over in his seat and wobbling back and forth. "He had some really good friends, too. They helped him every day even though he was all wrinkly."

"Oh," I said. "What happened to him?"

"This guy came along that was a Christian—well, there were two guys, I think. They came up to the wrinkled-up man and healed him, and now he's not all wrinkled up no more!"

"Uh, Son, I think you're talking about a man who was crippled up, not wrinkled up."

"Yeah, he got up and ran into the church and told everybody that all his wrinkles went away. Jesus healed him! He was so happy he started jumping around and stuff."

"Hmmm."

"Mommy, how'd that old man get all wrinkled up?"

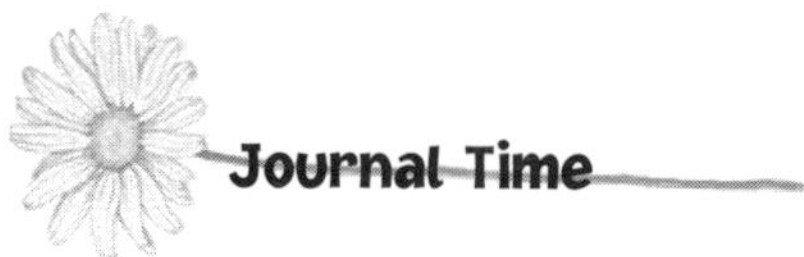

Journal Time

> Train up a child in the way he should go,
> And when he is old he will not depart from it...
> Foolishness is bound up in the heart of a child;
> The rod of correction will drive it far from him.
>
> —PROVERBS 22:6, 15

Father God, in Jesus' name I pray...

What are the "house rules" that you have established for your children to follow?

This chapter is "big" on discipline and instruction. Has the Lord shown you any changes that need to be made in either of these areas?

Sibling Rivalry 7

One of the greatest complaints from parents today is sibling rivalry. And the child who doesn't have siblings yet may be struggling to get along well when socializing with other children his age.

Just as our babies go through different stages of physical development, children also go through different stages of social development. At first, they are not equipped to be interactive with other children. The following are the basic stages our children experience during their social playtime:

- *Solitary play:* She plays by herself with objects.
- *Parallel play:* He is able to play near other children, sometimes using the same play objects. It is important to the child at this stage to be in close proximity to his siblings or playmates.
- *Cooperative play:* Children begin to interact, following one another into play, sharing toys and suggesting what they want to do next.
- *Social pretend play:* This is play that makes use of imaginary and symbolic objects, usually involving several children who pretend various social role models, such as policeman, teacher, knight, fireman or queen.

We need to be sure that our child has actually progressed to the cooperative play level before we place an expectation on them to show love in this area. Every child advances at a different pace, and I fully trust the Holy Spirit to nudge us when our son or daughter is ready for the next step of training.

I think the important thing here is that we relax and enjoy these stages and don't take their various aspects of development too seriously. It's good to be aware of what to expect and to hear God's voice on how to help them develop through the challenges of each stage of social play.

THE FABULOUS FOURS AND THE LOVE RULES

As our children grow into the wonderful fours and fives, their interest in a social life usually escalates. This is the age when they love to be with children their own age and show off their toys and lunch boxes. These are the years when we find ourselves not only training our own children, but their friends and playmates, too!

I like the way God lays things out. God declares that His love is the greatest rule, and anyone who loves God and people will do everything else right, too. I use this positive rule of love at our house, and I repeat it again whenever my children have playmates over:

1. Love God—Don't hurt God.
2. Love others—Don't hurt others. (And don't hurt things that belong to others.)
3. Love yourself—Don't hurt yourself.

God's love is the rule. One of the greatest verses to memorize concerning sibling rivalry is the good old Golden Rule: "'Love the Lord your God with all your heart and with all your soul and with all your strength and with all your mind'; and 'Love your neighbor as yourself'" (Luke 10:27, NIV).

One way to get this one deep down into their little hearts is to have them act it out. You can try this or make up actions of your own:

Love the Lord your God (clap out "Lord your God" with three hard claps)
With all your heart (point to heart)
Soul (I have them make a fist and put it at their tummy)
Strength (show your muscles; the more you ham it up, the

more they'll want to repeat it!)
And mind (point to head)
And LOVE your neighbor (on the word "love" squeeze hug the person beside you)
As yourself. (Hug themselves. It is vital that they learn to love themselves, too.)

Words in Gift Boxes

One day God "downloaded" a wonderful object lesson to me that I used in helping my children speak kind words.

Florence Littauer has written a book called *Silver Boxes: The Gift of Encouragement*. In short, this book advises adults to see their words as gifts they give to one another.[1] When I heard this teaching at a ladies' meeting, I decided to try it with my children. I showed them a shiny little silver package with a bright silver bow (actually a child's building block wrapped in foil or silver paper and bow). They wanted to know what was inside, and I told them that words were inside. And words are a gift we give to each other.

They looked a bit puzzled at first. Suddenly, the Holy Spirit gave me an idea about how to use this gift of words as an object lesson. (*Thank You, Holy Spirit!*)

I pulled out their little building blocks and stacked three blocks in two stacks, one stack for each of them, on our china cupboard. (Judah was too little to play, but Johnathan and Eden really enjoyed this one!)

I put the shiny, silver, block-sized "gift of words" between the little towers as a reminder of what the blocks represented. I told them that every time I heard one of them say something kind or polite to their brother or sister that day, I would put a building block on that person's tower. Then we talked about examples of what would be a nice thing to say to each other.

Then I told them that if I heard one of them say something mean, unkind or rude to their brother or sister, I would take a block off their tower.

At first they were very conscious of the building blocks and made great efforts to build on their towers. Later on in the day, they forgot about the blocks, and life proceeded as normal.

That's when the real fun began for me! This is a great game for boys because they are so competitive. As soon as I took a block off Johnathan's tower, he suddenly found a whole line of kind things to say to his sisters to build his tower up.

I continued the building block lesson for several days. When the enthusiasm for the idea died down, I pointed to the blocks and told the children, "When we encourage one another and say kind things, we build each other up. Your words built these towers to stand so tall, and your words build up people to stand tall, too."

Even after I put away the building blocks, the silver box sat on the china cupboard for a few months as a reminder to say kind words.

What really surprised me was that my children still remembered this lesson months later.

ACT IN THE OPPOSITE SPIRIT

Love is the rule. So what do we do when the rule is broken between our children?

For us, the most effective weapon against sibling rivalry has been to act in the opposite spirit. This takes a few more seconds than just yelling, "Stop hitting your brother," but it seems to have a longer lasting effect.

If I can't get to the bottom of the story over who did what (which is quite often), I will have the two quarrelers sit on the couch and hold hands. Then I set the timer on the microwave for a set number of minutes. Some parents call this a "time-out." (A good rule of thumb is to have a five-year-old sit for five minutes, a three-year-old sit for three minutes, and so on.) The timer doesn't start until they are both willing to hold hands in a nice manner. When the timer goes off, they have to hug each other and say they're sorry before they're allowed to get up.

This type of discipline requires them to act in the opposite spirit—love, love, love! When they first sit down, they're frowning and sometimes angry or teary. After holding hands for a few minutes, their emotions are usually calm, and once in a while they even giggle by the end of the time-out.

God's love is the greatest power in the universe. Love heals, love hopes, love sent Jesus to die for our sins. And love conquered death, hell and the devil. Guard love! God's love is not only the golden rule, but it is also your family's most precious possession. Love is one of the few things your family will take to heaven with them one day!

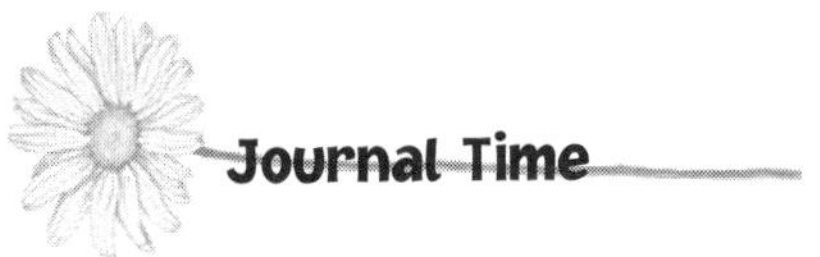

> Behold, how good and how pleasant it is
> For brethren [and sisters] to dwell together in unity.
>
> —Psalm 133:1

Father God, in Jesus' name I pray...

What are the positive ways in which your children interact and demonstrate their love for one another?

How can you help your children to develop more ways to encourage, help and show love to each other?

8 Bringing Them to Jesus

In chapter six I shared the necessity of teaching our children the Law of Moses and of giving them reasonable house rules to follow.

There's not an adult or child who is able to obey every rule every day for weeks or months on end. The good thing about the Law or established rules is that they show us right from wrong and expose our weaknesses, proving to us how desperately we need Jesus. Rules are tools! "The law was our tutor to bring us to Christ" (Gal. 3:24).

The Holy Spirit's Work in Salvation

The Holy Spirit will work with the Bible stories, values and boundaries you've taught your child to bring him to Jesus. Bringing people to Christ has been the Holy Spirit's job for two thousand years! He's more than capable—He's perfect.

Faith comes by hearing the Word of God. The Holy Spirit takes the Word of God that your child has heard and brings him to salvation. Jesus said of the Holy Spirit, "He will glorify Me, for He will take of what is Mine and declare it to you" (John 16:14).

Paul says the same thing. "Now we have received, not the spirit of the world, but the Spirit who is from God, that we might know the things that have been freely given to us by God" (1 Cor. 2:12). Basically, this means that the Holy Spirit knows what is in the heart of God and reveals the things of God to those who will listen.

Some people think that a child needs to come to complete conviction of sin before that child can truly be born again. While this may or may not be true, one thing is for sure—most preschool children aren't equipped to explain that type of conviction.

OK, let's uncomplicate all this with a couple of little stories.

"God Was Talkin' to Me"

Johnathan was three when he let me know he wanted to be born again. One day we were heading down the interstate highway when Johnathan spoke up from his car seat in the back of our car.

"I'm gonna be born soon."

"What?" I asked.

"I'm gonna be born soon."

"You mean born again?" I asked.

"Yeah, I'm gonna be born again soon."

"How do you know that?" I answered cautiously.

"God was talkin' to me," he answered simply.

I was intrigued. "He was? When did he talk to you?"

"Up in heaven. He said I'm gonna be born again soon."

"Praise God, Johnathan. Do you want to be born again?"

"Yup," he answered, nodding his head.

I briefly explained what that meant, but not at great length because God's hand was so strong on him. It seemed obvious that the Spirit of God was moving him to salvation. I didn't feel He needed my help or timing in the matter.

He asked me to read the Easter story to him that night. He asked me why it thundered and shook when Caiaphas was mean and Jesus died.

A day or so later he asked me, "Is Granddaddy born?"

"You mean born again? Yes, he's born again."

I did the hard thing. I waited for God's Spirit to bring him to the new birth.

I was cooking in the kitchen when he showed up at the doorway and announced, "We gotta obey, and one day we'll go to heaven, and you (Mom) are gonna come with us. God doesn't want sin in heaven, so we gotta obey our mom and dad and pick up our toys."

After he walked away, I cried at the sink. I felt so honored and blessed.

The next three weeks were spent going over John chapter 3. We talked about Nicodemus and being born again. I talked about Moses and the serpent on the pole, and explained that "sin hurts, and our sin hurt Jesus."

One night while he was sitting on my lap he said, "I want to born again right now."

So we went into his bedroom and knelt on the floor with Daddy. Johnathan admitted he had sinned and asked forgiveness and told God he wanted to be born again.

Wow! As a mother, I felt that I had labored in the birth process with my son all over again. And there he knelt, a brand-new baby in Christ. We all rejoiced!

I went into all of this detail because many parents want to try to understand the process of how they should lead a child to Christ. It's so important to give them the rules in the Word, the Jesus in the Word, and let the Holy Spirit do the work.

"I WANNA GET MARRIED"

Just yesterday I discovered that I need to really hear what it is my child is trying to communicate to me.

Eden will be four in a few months. Yesterday she was sitting on the couch when she suddenly started crying and said, "Mommy, I'm sad because I wanna get married, and now you won't let me."

Well, you can imagine how I laughed! I went into the speech about how she can't get married until she's a big girl, and all of that.

She was upset with me for laughing and told me, "It's not funny. You're hurting my feelings."

Hiding my giggles, I quickly apologized and set things right.

Later on, she told me, "I mean I want to be born."

"You mean born again?"

"Yes."

Well, wanting to be married is a good analogy of salvation, too. I just didn't understand, and Eden probably couldn't think of the right term. Three-year-olds have a hard time communicating what they want to say!

Of course, I let her know that she may ask Jesus into her life and be born again (married) whenever she is ready.

I should have caught the meaning of her "married" term because the day before she cried to me about being married. Eden came to me while I was on the phone and said, "Mommy, I have to tell you something."

She nagged until I put my hand over the receiver and said, "Eden, you know that it's rude to interrupt while Mommy's on the phone."

"But I want to tell you something!" She was crying by now.

"OK, what is it?"

"When we go to see Jesus (at a passion play next month), I'm gonna give my life to Jesus."

I felt so small. "Oh, Eden, that is important. Praise God."

When I finally got off the phone, she came up to me again and said, "I wanna do that because it's real down in my heart."

My Salvation Experience

When I was three and four years of age, my father would come home in the afternoon, and I would zoom over to the door and wildly hug him, pulling him to the couch saying, "Come on, Daddy, let's talk about important things."

Dad admitted being tired after work, and he wasn't always up to my big discussions. My mother often told me, "Sis, let your father get in the door first."

Yet these times were the delight of his heart, and today he still will ask me over the phone once in a while, "Well, Sis, do you want to come over and talk about important things?" Then he'll laugh warmly.

My parents and Sunday school teachers always talked about getting saved when I was three and four years of age. I remember thinking, *If getting saved is so great, and going to hell is so awful, how come nobody's asked me if I'm saved yet?*

I honestly began to think that no one really cared a whole lot about me. I waited and waited and waited for someone to ask me personally if I wanted to get saved. No one ever did.

Finally, I asked my mom if I could get saved. I remember feeling agitated that she wanted me to wait until my dad came home so he could pray with us, too.

I thought, *Boy, I'm never going to get saved.* (Dad may as well have been coming next month. An hour or two seems like a month or two to a little child.)

When Mom saw how eager I was, she knelt and prayed with me at the couch. I was a happy girl!

Don't Be Anxious

I hope these testimonies help you to see how parents can train children in the way of the Lord, then stay out of the way (hopefully not get in the way) while the Holy Spirit is working to bring your child to the Savior. Don't be anxious. It took time to birth your baby into this world, and it will take time to birth that baby into the next one!

In 1 Corinthians 7:14, Paul wrote advice to men and women who have children but are married to an unbelieving wife or husband:

> For the unbelieving husband is sanctified by the wife, and the unbelieving wife is sanctified by the husband; otherwise your children would be unclean, but now they are holy.

Even when just one parent is born again, your children are considered holy before God. What a wonderful promise!

May the God of Hope Fill You

I'm sure you'll agree with the apostle John, "I have no greater joy than to hear that my children walk in truth" (3 John 4). God is just. What you've sown by patiently training your child, you will richly reap.

"Train up a child in the way he should go, and when he is old

he will not depart from it" (Prov. 22:6). Believe God! And may His hope fill you with all joy and peace as you wait in faith for the rebirth of your child.

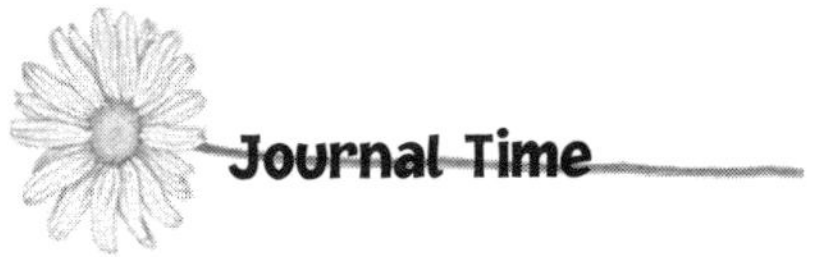

> Now may the God of hope fill you with all joy and peace in believing, that you may abound in hope by the power of the Holy Spirit.
>
> —Romans 15:13

Father God, in Jesus' name I pray…

Take a moment and jot down a sweet memory of a time your child has talked to you (or questioned you) about Jesus.

Does your child have a favorite Bible story? Do you see this Bible story bringing him closer to receiving Jesus as his Savior? Write your thoughts here.

9 Growing With Your Preschooler

Eden complained at the supper table that her leg hurt. (I think it was really an aversion to the pile of green vegetables she didn't want.) However, I rubbed her little leg and told her it was probably growing pains, which would go away.

At the mention of growing pains, Johnathan asked, "Mommy, does it hurt to grow up?"

The truth is, growing up doesn't have to hurt.

Children, who are totally dependent upon us at birth, begin the process of independence from us as early as two months, when they discover their little hand and are able to console themselves.

Around nine months of age the baby begins to crawl or "cruise" around furniture, discovering a world apart from the helping hands of Mom and Dad.

By the time your baby is six to eight months of age, he won't need a 3 A.M. feeding with a hearty burp every four ounces. He'll be feeding himself.

As much as we love holding our little princess, she'll never learn to crawl unless we put her down. And soon she'll probably prefer not to be carried from room to room, opting to crawl or cruise around the furniture instead.

It gets better. By the time they're nine to twelve months old, they understand the word *no*. From infancy to young adulthood the parent will be engaged in continual phases of letting go, while challenging the child to become responsible for himself. Whatever phase of growth our child is in, we must be willing to change with him and to encourage his independence.

Just Like Mommy and Daddy

Have you noticed that a child is much more eager to help sweep the floor at age two than at age ten? There's a good reason for that. God placed within small children a sensitive learning period, which really should be utilized by parents. After all, those little tykes really just want to be like Mommy and Daddy!

Why does a baby want to learn to walk? It is because that baby has watched Mom and Dad walking around him all the time.

Why does a toddler want to help you sort laundry in her own little way? Because she has watched Mommy fold that laundry and put it away dozens of times!

Small children watch and often follow their mothers from room to room as they work to keep the household running. Most of the time they want to be right in the middle of the floor when you're vacuuming or in the laundry basket into which you are putting the freshly folded clothes!

Self-Esteem

A desire accomplished is sweet to the soul.

—Proverbs 13:19

We all feel a sense of satisfaction when we have accomplished a task and can stand back and look at a job well done. Children need that sense of accomplishment as well. Small children who learn to complete practical chores have a great start on self-esteem.

Of course, a three-year-old won't dust the living room or sweep the floor as thoroughly as Mom or Dad. But there's nothing like the triumph of a three-year-old announcing, "Look, I did it all by myself!"

Teach your children when they're young and interested in helping you. Remember, giving a child a chore to do not only lifts a burden from us, but also it teaches them how to be responsible for themselves and to reach their full potential.

CHORES PREPARE THEM FOR SCHOOL

My son's kindergarten teacher has a bachelor of science degree in secondary education with a minor in early childhood development. Recently she told me, "Many children, when they come into kindergarten, don't know how to be responsible for themselves. They tend to lack simple skills like persevering to the end to pick up their toys or to complete their seatwork."

She said it's tough at the beginning of the year when there are some children who are able to stick with a task and others who must be continually prodded.

Because children watch their parents go to work, they should easily understand when we tell them that they're going to school to work. We should expect them to work and encourage their achievements.

"It's really better if a parent doesn't jump in to *help* his or her child complete simple tasks," his teacher told me. "I can always tell when a child has had good training in simple chores or tasks at home. That will be the child who completes his seatwork, has a longer attention span and excels in classroom jobs."

READY FOR CHANGE

The mother or father who is sensitive to his or her child and to the Holy Spirit can sense when that child is ready for a change or a new challenge. For instance, my daughter Eden is three. At certain times this year she will be ready to master various independent skills by herself. She will accomplish skills like putting on her coat by herself, buttoning her shirt, hopping on one foot, taking her clothes off for a bath, putting at least some of them on by herself and recognizing her own name printed on paper.

Knowing when she is ready to learn a new task can be difficult. The best time to teach her to put on her coat is not when I'm in a rush to get her brother off to school. Those "hurry up" times are probably the worst time to teach her anything except, "Obey Mommy so we can get Johnathan to school on time."

If I tried to teach her all of these skills every day we would both end up frustrated. It's wonderful to flow in the grace of God after praying for God's method and order when training my children.

I've heard it said that more things are caught than taught. I agree. Seize the moment. Make the most of the opportunities that present themselves throughout the day. When they need help with a zipper, make the most of the moment—don't see it as an interruption. While their desire to learn is strong, teach them the first step or two in zipping.

Education From the Dishwasher and Bathtub!

Just as the pots and pans and instrument basket encourage children to sing and play and dance, some inexpensive plastic bowls can enhance their ability to sort. One of the things your child will learn in kindergarten is sorting and patterns. You can get him off to a good start by buying colorful plastic cereal bowls! It's great if you can buy colorful bowls of the same size in one set and then smaller colored bowls in another set. We like to use the smaller bowls for salsa, vegetable dip and portable snacks.

When a child is three or four, she is able to help you put away clean dishes from the dishwasher. You're actually teaching her an educational skill when you show your child how to put the right lid on the right Tupperware container! Not only is she learning to help, but she is also learning to sort.

Using bowls of the same size and shape but varied colors gives children the opportunity to sort and stack in a pattern all their own. You will need at least two to four blue, two to four green, and others in order for your child to make varied patterns. Of course, this can be done with plastic tumblers or assorted napkins, too.

Eden loves to put the bowls away. She always shows me her stack of bowls and says, "Mommy, look, I made a pattern." She often forgets about the dishes and sits in the middle of the floor playing with the bowls for a while.

Preschoolers love the water. In addition to a few large water toys, we buy foam letters, which can be found in most department or dollar stores. Even a two-year-old can learn to identify the first letter of his name. Whenever I would put one of my children of that age into the tub, I would hold up the first letter of that child's name and ask, "What is this called?"

This little game takes only about forty-five seconds. We would progress to the second letter after a while, and soon that child's entire name would be in the bathtub with him or her. The foam letters stick to the side of the tub, so it's easy for them to arrange the letters of their name.

These foam letters are fun in the wading pool, too.

THREE TYPES OF LEARNERS

There are basically three types of learners: visual learners, auditory learners and kinesthetic learners.

1. Visual learner—A visual learner learns best when he sees a picture or, when old enough, can read the words on paper. Some of my students in first grade progressed very slowly until they learned to read fluently. One student in particular went from a C average in all classes to an A average across the board simply because he could read and therefore comprehend what I wrote on the board or pointed to on a chart. For this child, seeing was not only believing—it was learning!

2. Auditory learner—This student can hear you say something today and still quote your words a week later. I had one student who was outstanding in this type of learning. It was very difficult for him to process putting words onto paper or to look at words and sound them out. He literally failed many of his written papers. But when I taught something orally, he could recite it back to me in

greater detail than all his classmates. Although we had to continue to help him process from hearing to pencil and paper, his confidence soared as I called on him in oral lessons.

3. Kinesthetic learner—This student may appear to need entertaining more than an education. An inexperienced teacher or parent may feel some exasperation at teaching her. The truth is, she has to have her hands on the subject matter, feeling it with her fingers or experiencing it as much as possible. One little girl I know could not recognize or write her letters until her teacher had her write them in a little shoe box of sand in the classroom. At home, this child needed to trace her letters with her mother on a washcloth as she took a bath or use Lincoln Logs to build her letters. There is something about the touch and the experience that makes it stick. One more word about these students—sometimes they can learn an auditory or visual lesson if you allow them simply to finger an interesting button or necklace or a soft fuzzy sweater while you are teaching.

Most of us are a combination of two or three of these learning methods, with one type of learning more dominant than the others. That's why it's important that we provide children visuals such as pictures and books, auditory prompts such as music and read-aloud books on tape, and lots of manipulative practice with puzzles, sort and stack toys, and foam letters and numbers for those kinesthetic learners.

Taking Care of Their Clothes

There are some practical things we have done to challenge our preschoolers to gain independence and accept more responsibility. At bedtime, we diapered the little tykes and helped them put on their pajamas. Once they had been walking for several months and carrying toys to and fro, they were able to take their dirty clothes to the hamper in the evening.

We walked with them to the hamper with clothes in hand the first few times until they had the hang of it. (Lights have to be on or this plan will not work.)

While walking, we spoke the direction such as, "Susie, take your clothes to the hamper." After a few times, our child began to relate the command with the action of throwing the clothes in the hamper. Always, always, always, we praised our children for any efforts they made toward that hamper.

PUT IT WHERE THEY CAN REACH IT

At age three, Eden was old enough to pull her pajamas out of her drawer before bedtime. The only problem was that her pajama drawer was too high for her to reach. I know this sounds simple, but we switched her drawers. It took less than five minutes to put the drawers she uses the most on the bottom where she can reach them.

Then I went through the action. I asked her to put away a pair of pajamas I had in my hand. I showed her how to pull and push the drawer properly so it will shut completely. Now she's able to complete that task herself.

Five-year-old Johnathan is old enough now to begin pouring his own cereal (and baby Judah's old enough to crawl up on the table to help him). I decided to put the cereal bowls and cereal boxes within his reach. I like to buy several quarts of milk instead of the big one-gallon containers. The ones with the handles on them make it easy for him to lift and maneuver the milk by himself.

After the cereal bowls and cups were switched to a lower cupboard, I recruited both my three- and five-year-old to help unload the dishwasher. (Mom puts away sharp knives and glasses.)

Of course, the day came when Johnathan decided he really

didn't like helping to unload the dishwasher. So, one morning we opened our Bibles and quoted the "Mommy Version" of Colossians 3:23: "Work hard and happy in all you do as though you're working for the Lord."

Many times we have quoted that scripture while scrambling around the kitchen together, putting away the dishes or setting the table. I'm amazed at how much we love to work together at that small chore!

Little people are usually willing and certainly able to hang up their little coats. We found a pegboard at a yard sale and painted it. We hung the board on the middle of the children's closet door and gave them the responsibility of hanging up their jackets, book bags and pocketbooks. You could also use inexpensive plastic hook sets for doors, which you can find in the domestic section of most department stores.

Little ones can learn to give themselves a bath. One day when I was busily bathing my third little preschooler, a friend who was visiting told me how the four preschoolers for whom she babysat bathed themselves.

"Really?" I asked. It didn't seem possible.

So I tried it. I was thrilled to find out that, with a little practice, my four-year-old could wash himself from head to toe.

His new skill didn't give me the liberty to leave the room, but it did give me a few moments to clean the rest of the bathroom. Most of our bath times are unhurried so they can play and I can clean. If the sink and toilet are clean, I'll take the time to sit on the floor by the tub and read or call a friend.

I was amazed that he was able to learn to wash, always beginning with "face first," then covering each territory, top to bottom, doing the feet last.

Self-bathing is a process. Now three-year-old Eden can do most of her bath except for washing her hair. My five-year-old can wash his hair, but sometimes he needs assistance to rinse out his bangs.

Household chores can be a shared family event that will

provide your preschooler with self-esteem and a great sense of accomplishment. And sharing the workload will leave everyone with more time to enjoy each other!

Journal Time

A desire accomplished is sweet to the soul.

—PROVERBS 13:19

Father God, in Jesus' name I pray…

What is your little one's favorite household chore?

What kind of learner do you think your child might be (visual, auditory or kinesthetic)? In what ways has your child shown that this is his strength?

10 Booting Up a Prayer "Program"

Have you ever thought, *How can I pray when it's difficult to find fifteen minutes to shower in the morning?* I have! Prayer is one of those areas that most people feel guilty about. How much prayer is enough? What if I lose my preschooler's interest and attention? What if I lose attention myself?

Prayer is a catchall term for conversation with God, petition to God and thanksgiving to God. Some people think living life in the Spirit is having daily "devotions," where we read the Bible and pray once a day. Not so. True life in the Spirit is an ongoing talk with God.

When I had my first baby, I looked with envy at people who prayed every day for an hour or so. I wanted to do that, but I found myself sleeping at every available moment and not praying.

I cried out often to God, "Lord, can You show me how to walk in the Spirit while I'm raising babies? Is there anybody who has actually walked in the Spirit while training small children?"

God showed me that He understands each busy season we're in and wants to be in it with us, to help us with His grace and wisdom. And yes, it is possible to walk in the Spirit while raising busy, noisy toddlers and preschoolers!

As God directed me, I found that my prayer life took on the new form of talking with God throughout my day rather than large blocks of "rending the heavens." When my children were infants, I prayed while I nursed them. In fact, I often received worship songs or children's poems during those times. As they grew (and my sleep settled back into six or seven hours a night), I found other spare moments to pray.

When I talk to God throughout my day, it doesn't take me as

long to reach heaven later on. My goal is to keep my heart in tune with God throughout the day so that when I finally do get a few minutes to go to God alone, it doesn't take me half an hour to get my prayers past the ceiling.

"Booting Up" a Prayer Program

Because a preschooler is still learning to form words and sentences, prayer is one of the easiest "programs" to "boot up." (Hope you don't mind the computer language here.) Let me explain.

Although bedtime prayers with preschoolers are great, "through-the-day" prayers are better. For instance, breakfast is a good time to say, "Good morning, Lord. I love You..." Then continue to bless the food, giving the children the opportunity to pray if they'd like to. This approach to God makes Him more real to everyone than repetitious blessings over food.

While I'm pulling out vitamins, sometimes I look up and say, "Thank You, God, for these beautiful children You've given me. God, I am so blessed." I'll look over at them to find them grinning from ear to ear.

It's good just to start the day praying for protection and for God to order your day with His plans and not your own. You can pray while changing a diaper, driving the car or throwing in a load of laundry. If you stop to kneel every time you talk to God, either you will stop praying or stop working. God doesn't mind if you send up your petitions while you work. As parents, we talk to each other while we work, don't we?

If you stay connected with God by conversational prayer throughout your day, you will be sensitive to pray when opportunity knocks. And prayer is not so superspiritual. Sometimes it comes out, "Lord, give me patience, please." At other times when I feel overwhelmed with a particular behavior I see in my children, I'll pray, "Lord, show me something from Your Word that I can teach my children to help them ________ [work together, play together, share, whatever]."

Prayer Images

Speaking of examples, you can find wonderful pictures of children praying by shopping at Christian bookstores, department stores or yard sales. I found an inexpensive one at an outlet store that showed a boy praying with his warring angel, Jesus and the Father standing behind the boy. I put that one in Johnathan's room.

We have a picture in our dining room of a man and woman praying in a field they had obviously just harvested. We point to it sometimes before prayer and explain how we need to give thanks to God for the food we receive.

This is sort of a review on offering godly images to our children, but displaying a simple picture that shows prayer in your home can be very effective.

One day as I was busily going from one room to the next, cleaning up dirty socks and scattered toys, I noticed two-year-old Judah in her bedroom, looking up at a picture of Jesus with children on His lap. One of the children had light-colored hair, like Judah, and had her hands folded while she was looking up at Jesus.

I scooped up little Judah and pointed to the picture. "Look, Honey, that little girl looks like Judah. See? She has her hands folded, and she's praying to Jesus! Does Judah like to pray to Jesus?"

Judah just stared and then nodded her head. I kissed her cheek, swung her back down to the floor and continued my cleaning.

I was heading for the kitchen when Johnathan ran to me and said, "Mom! Guess what? You'll never believe what Judah's doing."

"Oh, no," I said. "Let me guess..."

"No, Mom. She's being good! Come see!"

I followed Johnathan back to Judah's room to find her squatting beside her dresser, surrounded by baby strollers she had placed around herself. Her little hands were folded tightly and her eyes squeezed shut, and she was earnestly praying in nonstop baby talk. Every once in a while I heard "Jesus" as she prayed. I was truly taken back.

Now, before you get too impressed, let me add that the very next day that little princess hid behind our recliner and unloaded an entire large jar of Vaseline all over herself, the carpet and the recliner. (Her grandmother insists she has a bit of her mother in her.)

Still, that one moment with the picture and little Judah has borne much fruit. Sometimes we kneel together around the bunk bed and pray before bedtime. During those times, little Judah will yell, "I pray, I pray!!"

During one of those prayer sessions, Daddy told her, "OK, fold your hands."

Judah's little face contorted and strained with great effort as she pushed her hands together. With eyes clamped shut, she rattled off a row of nonstop baby talk to her Maker.

She prattled on and on until her older sister grew impatient and said, "Amen," before Judah was actually finished!

Daddy and I stifled a giggle, then pointed out to the older two children that little Judah just led us all in a sweet example of fervent prayer. And while we couldn't understand it, God heard every word.

Deuteronomy 6:7 says that we are to teach our children as we sit, walk, lie down and rise up. I wasn't preparing a Sunday school lesson the day Judah prayed; I was just cleaning up messy rooms! Again, we can pray and enjoy interaction with our God as we go about our daily responsibilities.

PRAY FIRST

When your child hurts her knee, the first thing she does is run to you. The best thing you can do is run to your parent, Daddy God. First, pray over that "boo-boo" or "owie," and then reach for the ice or Band-Aid. It's a simple plan, but the implications go deep into your child's soul, showing her that the first place Mom and Dad go when they're hurting is to God.

Sometimes when my two-year-old bangs her toe, I'll ask her older sister to pray for her. Eden sends up a simple prayer, and Judah is often satisfied at that and runs off to play.

When a child is frustrated at picking up toys or completing a task, I'll often lay my hand on that child's little head and pray, "Grace to you, Honey, in Jesus' name." Grace is God's ability to help them in their work. (I also try to be sure the task at hand is within their capabilities.)

If you're like us, you probably have those days when it seems that confusion reigns instead of Jesus. No one seems happy with their shoes, their cereal or their toys. If I'm in over my head (which is more often than I would like to be), I pray. I'll call the children over to me, sit down with them and pray aloud. They hear me pouring out my frustration to God instead of to them, and they see by example that Mommy goes to God when she doesn't know what to do.

I watched with amazement one day as Johnathan's kindergarten teacher told her wild and out-of-order class, "Let's all stop now and put our hand right here (on the tummy or chest) and speak peace to ourselves." Those little "cherubs" obeyed, and, you know, it worked! They suddenly stopped where they were, placed their little hands over their chests or tummies and said, "Peace." It wasn't exactly a prayer, but just speaking the promises from the Bible over themselves.

The World in Their Hearts

Every once in a while we will pray for a missionary or even for an entire country. I keep pictures of missionaries from church brochures, Internet printouts and magazine cuttings on our refrigerator. From time to time one of them will ask, "Who's that?" I'll explain what it means to be a missionary in another country.

It helps to have a household globe to put on the floor during prayer time. I like to help my children point to the country for which they are praying, or I show them the country where the missionary for whom they are praying lives.

Yes, I'm one of those parents who reminds my little ones that we have very much in our country and that the Bible tells us that if we have two coats, we should give one to someone else who needs one. If we have food to eat, we should share. I want my children to realize they are a part of a very big and very needy world that God loves.

THE PRAYER EXAMPLE

You probably already know this, but let me just say it and throw in a great story, OK?

Children learn more by our example than we can imagine. There, I said it! My friend told me a story about her four-year-old, Ellie, who went to visit her grandmother.

Ellie's grandmother tucked her into bed, and Ellie said her prayers, asking God to help Grandma become a Christian. Grandma was quite upset with Ellie's mom and dad, thinking they told their little daughter that Grandma wasn't a Christian!

She asked Ellie, "Why don't you think I am a Christian?"

Ellie answered, "Well, I have never heard you pray, and I have never seen you read your Bible, and I have never seen you at church. So I thought you weren't a Christian."

The reason that Jesus' disciples asked, "Lord, teach us to pray," is because they saw from His example that Jesus' powerful ministry was preceded by prayer and fellowship with His Father.

The same holds true with our children. A child who sees his parent pray and read her Bible will deem it important enough to try it himself.

A couple of times a week I will get up early to pray. Johnathan will often ask me, "Mommy, when you get up to pray and read the Bible, get me up. I want to pray with you."

I have done that a few times and enjoyed our times together. Most of the time I need to be alone, though, and I let him sleep.

The best thing you can do for your prayer life is not to live in condemnation over it. God sees and knows the demands of preschool parenting. He is happy to help us if we just stay connected in conversation throughout our day, ready to obey if He calls us aside from time to time for longer periods of prayer and quiet time with Him.

Our many prayers don't impress Him, anyway. It's our fellowship that He wants.

Written prayers

Since we're this close to the journal time, I want to reiterate the power of a parent's prayers, especially when some of those prayers are written down for future generations to see them.

I am so thankful that when God wrote the accounts of great biblical heroes like Isaac, Solomon, Samuel, John and especially Jesus, He included a word about the faith and prayers of their respective parents. During stressful seasons of raising preschoolers, I read the prayers of these saints to gain strength and a sense of hope and destiny for my child.

David wrote:

> I will make Your name to be
> remembered in all generations;
> Therefore the people shall praise
> You forever and ever.
>
> —Psalm 45:17

David's vision went beyond his own family. He was able to foresee the impact his faith in God would have on his grandchildren, reverberating through the generational line.

Aren't you encouraged to know that men and women of God like Sarah, Hannah, David, Zacharias and Elizabeth have prayed over their children?

Many single mothers worry about the lack of a father's influence in their children's lives. I told you about Mary Ball Washington, mother of George Washington, in the introduction to this book. She wasn't a child psychologist or even a soccer mom—but she was a praying mother. And with God's help, after the death of her husband, she raised their children by herself. George was only eleven years old when his father died, yet this boy who had no father was used by God to be the father of this great nation! Why? God Himself was George Washington's father.

Mary Ball Washington and her son George knew how to touch God with their prayers. Mary's advice to her son when he was sent off to battle was simply, "Remember that God only is our sure trust. To Him, I commend you. My son, neglect not the duty of secret prayer."

George did pray. One of the most famous paintings of George Washington shows him kneeling in the snow in prayer at Valley Forge where many of his men fell sick from near starvation and frigid cold. George valued prayer so much that he even kept a prayer diary that has been read by generations of Americans that followed him, revealing to the readers a truly devoted life of prayer. I believe that prayer put George in total fellowship with his heavenly Father who kept him and watched over him better than any earthly father could have.

Every time I think of George Washington as a young adult kneeling at his mother's rocking chair while she prayed over him before he left home, my heart soars with greater expectation when I pray for my own children. Later, when they are adults about to go out into the big world, I have the wonderful hope that they will see the value of their mother's rocking-chair prayers.

Perhaps you haven't had a moment to write down a prayer before today. Why not start now? You may want to buy a little journal when you're finished with this book and continue to jot down important prayers and thoughts for your child.

Journal Time

> Call to Me, and I will answer you, and show you great and mighty things, which you do not know.
>
> —JEREMIAH 33:3

Father God, in Jesus' name I pray…

Take some time to write a prayer of blessing for your children, listing the biblical blessings and promises you want God to bring into your children's lives.

Have some fun! Point to a "prayer picture" in your home, whether on the wall, television or in a picture book. Explain the meaning of the picture and pray with your child. How did he respond?

11 Don't Forget to Rest!

When Moses returned to his people after meeting with God on the mountaintop, God made an entrance! And what did He have to say? It was the first time He ever spoke the Ten Commandments to His people. (Later on He wrote them down for Moses to give to the people—just so the rest of us wouldn't forget them!)

> Now all the people witnessed the thunderings, the lightning flashes, the sound of the trumpet, and the mountain smoking; and when the people saw it, they trembled and stood afar off.
>
> —Exodus 20:18

When joyfully obeyed, one of these commandments will bring a framework of grace and divine order to your family's entire week.

You may be thinking, *Yeah, the one about honoring your father and mother*. Or maybe you believe it is, "Don't commit adultery."

Those two are certainly vital to family harmony. But there's one command—the fourth—that was written to rejuvenate our spirit, soul and body.

God suggested—no, He *commanded*—His people to meet with Him once a week and to make that day a holy day of rest.

In the New Testament Paul admonishes us, "Let us not give up meeting together, as some are in the habit of doing, but let us encourage one another—and all the more as you see the Day approaching" (Heb. 10:25, NIV).

A Day to Set Our Affections

Even in this century, the Sabbath day, which most churches celebrate on Sunday because our Lord was resurrected on a Sunday, needs to be a day that we set aside to meet with our God.

Eden is three right now. Every day she asks us (no exaggeration), "Are we going to church?" If the answer is *yes*, she giggles and claps her little hands.

If the answer is *no*, she responds, "Aw, why not?" or "Yes, it is. Please? I want to go."

Church is our number one place to go. If we sense that some other entertainment, sport or outing has too much of the children's attention, we slowly withdraw from that activity until it has less hold on them. I try to keep a check on my own affections too, following Paul's advice: "Set your affection on things above, not on things on the earth" (Col. 3:2, KJV).

One word concerning church—the nursery, toddler and preschool classes at your church should be an anticipated joy for both you and your child. The nursery should tingle with love, acceptance and gentleness toward your baby.

With the exception of the "no-no war" stage, or perhaps a clinging season when your child doesn't want to go with anyone else but you, your preschool child should enjoy going to his or her classroom.

Does your child's classroom teacher meet you and your child with a smile? Does she or he seem excited about working with preschoolers? Some churches are so short-staffed that they rely on teenagers to be your child's primary teacher. A mature teen can do a great job. But it should be a warning sign to you if, when you arrive at the classroom door, you find teenagers standing around talking to one another—not to the students—just before class starts. Your child most likely will not be getting the best in his or her church experience from that teen-managed classroom.

Parents have a right to expect qualified help in preschool classes. If you do not find that in your church, ask why. Work to change things, and offer to help where you can. If all else fails, visit other churches to see the differences in your child's care during church. You may need to consider changing churches.

MADE FOR OUR BENEFIT

For our family, observing the fourth commandment involves more than packing up the family and going to church. We always try to set aside part of the day to rest from the normal activities of the week. In the afternoon, it's naptime for everyone. (Now that Johnathan is five, sometimes he will look at his picture Bible and pray during that time.) We hang out at home, spending larger blocks of time in the Word individually and as a family.

Jesus said that God made the Sabbath for our benefit. Although it's hard to put on the brakes, we discipline ourselves to slow down and set apart the day to rest in the Word and rest our bodies. It's amazing how our whole week of work benefits from that one day of rest.

For me, it's become a matter of need, obedience and joy. Sometimes I'm so exhausted by the end of the week that I'm hungry for a day set apart to rest in God. At other times, it's hard to set aside my writing, shopping, laundry and household cares. But that's the principle of the Sabbath. If I make that day, the Sabbath, truly the Lord's day, the rest of my week flows under a greater grace because I'm filled up with physical, mental and spiritual rest.

Sometimes fellowship can play an important role in the day of rest. As long as we make it a "Mary" day and not a "Martha" day, fellowship can be of great benefit. (See Luke 10:38–42.)

PREPARING TO MEET WITH GOD

The most important thing is to be in the spiritual place that God wants your family to be. Church can be a wonderful family event if everyone is rested and prepared to meet his God in a corporate meeting. It takes work to keep the peace when every family member is getting dressed to go to church. We teach our little ones that it's good to dress up for Jesus, and we like to honor him by giving Him our best.

Of course, it's also true that God will gladly accept us in blue jeans and leather jackets. I dress up because I want to. It's just another part of my worship of the Lord.

We Just Do It

Dressing up is a matter of personal preference. It's not one of the commandments! After the rush to get everybody ready and buckled into car seats, we head off to church. One of us usually starts the singing, preparing our hearts to receive from God. We really don't *teach* the Sabbath principle as much as we *just do it*. If it means something to us, it will mean something to them.

If we're observing the Sabbath because we have to, our children know it, and soon they'll go just out of obligation, their hearts far from God. If we're observing the Sabbath because it's in our hearts to do so, our children will find it easy to submit to that, and it will be a wonderful, beneficial routine built into their lives.

There's much to be taught on the subject of taking a day of rest. If you look up the word *Sabbath* in the back of your Bible, you'll find plenty of verses to refer to. This is one of those areas where God may lead families to observe the Lord's day in many different ways. I'm only sharing here what works (joyfully) for us.

The Sabbath Was Made for Man

Please bear in mind what Jesus had to say about the Lord's day in Mark 2:27: "The Sabbath was made for man, and not man for the Sabbath." The Sabbath truly was made for people! The God who created us made a cycle of work and rest that meets the needs of our spirits, souls and bodies. Praise the Almighty!

Our spirits need fine-tuned, clear connections with our Maker, Lord and Friend.

Our souls need to draw near to God to regain any sensitivity to Him or others that may have been lost throughout the week.

Our minds need time to process a week's worth of information, organizing clear direction for the week ahead.

Our bodies need to rest.

STEP OUT

Truly, there are fewer and fewer Christians who really know how to rest. If you desire this principle of Sabbath to be worked into your family, trust God to meet you as you step out in faith to observe His fourth command.

One step at a time, God will reveal to you what will benefit you and your family the most.

> Remember the Sabbath day, to keep it holy. Six days you shall labor and do all your work, but the seventh day is the Sabbath of the Lord your God...Therefore the Lord blessed the Sabbath day and hallowed it.
>
> —EXODUS 20:8–11

Father God, in Jesus' name I pray...

What special ways has your family developed for incorporating a day of rest into your family life?

If you have not taken time before this to think of some creative ways for your family to celebrate God's day of rest, perhaps you would like to sit down together as a family now and develop a plan you can follow for celebrating the Sabbath as a family.

When My Child Needs Healing 12

If I'm going to buy a new appliance, I like to choose one with a big warranty. I can trust someone who says the new dryer I bought has a five-year, unlimited guarantee. And if that dryer starts dishing out wet, turned-over clothes, the first thing I'll do is call the company who made it and ask them to fix it.

The same thing applies to health and healing. If my body or my child's body needs to be maintained or repaired, the first practical thing to do is to call the One who made that body in the first place and ask Him to fix it or give me wisdom on how to use it correctly.

No one else has better expertise on my new dryer than the company that made it, and no one else has better expertise on our body mechanisms than the God who made them. I don't want to oversimplify here, but calling on the Creator is really the practical thing to do.

God's answer to "fixing" my body may be a supernatural healing. God wrote His healing warranties in Scripture.

Our Bodies' Warranties

> Bless the Lord, O my soul,
> And forget not all His benefits:
> Who forgives all your iniquities,
> Who heals all your diseases.
>
> —Psalm 103:2–3

> And the prayer of faith will save the sick, and the Lord will raise him up. And if he has committed sins, he will be forgiven.
>
> —James 5:15

> Who Himself bore our sins in His own body on the tree, that we, having died to sins, might live for righteousness—by whose stripes you were healed.
>
> —1 PETER 2:24

SUPERNATURAL HEALING

Johnathan was three years old when he hurt his hip after jumping off the stool in our living room. He limped around a little, and we prayed, looking for a healthy little boy the next morning. Johnathan woke up in the middle of the night and cried out in pain.

The next day his limp grew worse until he had to be carried everywhere, and he would just sit and stare when we put him down. I took him to the pediatrician, who quickly determined a hip injury and ordered x-rays. By this time I had to carry Johnathan everywhere, and he would cry out if we picked him up the wrong way. I carried him from the car to the doctors' offices, into the bathroom, back to the car and into the house.

At home, Johnathan sat and stared. Now, I'm sure you can imagine your three-year-old just quietly sitting on the couch all day long. The x-rays came back that nothing was wrong.

Johnathan's hip looked normal. I thought, *Then why is my three-year-old sitting and staring if there's nothing wrong?*

My compassion was great for my son, and I sought God further concerning his healing. The Holy Spirit prompted me to go play the piano and sing. About the same time, Johnathan stretched his arms out to me and said, "Hold me, Mommy." (Daddy was mowing the lawn.)

I held him for a moment, but the urgency for me to play and sing became stronger. I said, "Honey, I believe the Holy Spirit is telling me to sing and play the piano."

"I don't want to sing and play an instrument. Hold me!"

It was tough, but I felt like I had to listen to God, not listen to Johnathan. I sat him on the stool beside the piano and sat down to play and sing "O the Blood of Jesus," "God Didn't Give Me a Spirit of Fear" and "There's Power in the Blood."

By now Johnathan was upset and crying. I said, "Honey, try to get up and walk."

"I can't," he wailed. Suddenly he quieted, and I continued to sing, choking back tears of compassion for my little boy. Johnathan stood up and took a little step. Encouraged by his tiny step of faith, I sang with all my heart, and Johnathan limped out two more steps while holding on to the furniture.

"Look, I'm healed, Mommy," he said. "Jesus is healing me!" By the end of the song he still had a limp but wasn't holding on to the furniture. "Look, I'm healed, I'm healed, Mommy! Go get Daddy!"

The next day he said to me, "Mommy, Jesus is healing me. I can walk, but I can't dance yet!" Johnathan became progressively better, day by day.

Consult the Creator

The God who knit us together in our mother's womb, blew His breath into the first man and fashioned a woman out of a rib is often the last one to be consulted when the body breaks down. Why is that?

We must be sensible in areas of health and healing. I used to run my children to the pediatrician at the drop of a hat. I wanted my children to be healthy, and I honestly felt I was being a good mother by taking them right away. Lately, my approach is to go to God first—God the Creator, Jesus the Healer and the Holy Spirit who gives gifts of healing and guides me in what to do.

Johnathan's miraculous healing strengthened everyone's faith. I was left wondering why nothing showed up on the x-rays, but blessed that God had definitely healed my son.

The Body—Created to Heal Itself

Johnathan's five now, and two months ago he was dancing like David (OK, like a wild man) all over the living room floor during an upbeat family praise session. His hip hurt when he climbed the ladder to his bunk.

Of course, Mom's thinking, *Not again.*

The next morning Johnathan woke up in great pain. He wasn't able to climb down the bunk bed ladder and needed help getting to the bathroom and the breakfast table. Within the last year I had started seeing doctors of chiropractic for my own hip trouble, which I had acquired in my last pregnancy.

This time I bypassed x-rays for Johnathan (since they didn't show anything before), and I took him to my chiropractor, Dr. Kevin Jackson. I explained how Johnathan injured his hip. Dr. Jackson checked my son, looking for any misalignments that may cause interference to the nervous system. He closely examined the length of his legs, checked his spine and measured the temperature on his neck with a painless little device that looks like an ear thermometer.

Immediately he saw the problem. He adjusted Johnathan's hip area, and within one minute, Johnathan got up and walked around without any limp. The doctor said he might experience some soreness for a day or so. Johnathan told me that after lunch at school he had no pain at all and played with his friends on the playground at recess.

When God made our bodies, He made them to heal themselves. Dr. Kevin Jackson explains it this way: "The Power that created the body heals the body. Your body has the ability to heal itself of any disease known to mankind if it's functioning properly. If you cut your hand and it heals, you just witnessed the principle of self healing."

My point in sharing all of this is that through the trauma of two hip injuries, God healed my son. The first time, it was the supernatural work of faith in the blood of Jesus—Johnathan was healed by the stripes laid on Jesus when the Savior was beaten. The second time, it was a natural work that included faith in the power of the Creator, who made Johnathan's body to heal itself.

If you're wondering how chiropractic care works, I'm not a

good teacher in this field. I can tell you that Dr. Jackson's approach to healthcare is to search for a cure by trying the natural first, medicine second and surgery last.

It bears repeating that although we use the natural means that God placed on the earth for our body's maintenance and healing, our faith should not rest in His creation (the natural realm), but in Him, the Creator. He is the embodiment of health and healing, and His Holy Spirit directs us as to the course we should pursue when we are seeking healing for our child or ourselves. I say, "Go to God first, and get out those Scripture warranties."

Antibiotics, Ear Infections and Prayer

Johnathan's testimony applies to the healing of bones. You may be thinking, *Yeah, but what about those nasty ear infections and viruses?*

The other day, I picked up a brochure from my pediatrician's office that is put out by the American Academy of Pediatrics. It is titled, "Your Child and Antibiotics—Unnecessary Antibiotics CAN Be Harmful."

This brochure states, "Each time we take antibiotics, sensitive bacteria are killed, but resistant ones may be left to grow and multiply. The more antibiotics prescribed, the higher the chance that your child will be infected with resistant bacteria."

I would like to explain this phenomenon in another testimony. My daughter Eden had several ear infections last year. Hating to see her in pain, I immediately took her to the pediatrician, who automatically prescribed an antibiotic. Of course, the infection left, but within three weeks, another ear infection developed. Medical doctors will tell you that this is common.

It is a medically known fact that the antibiotic fights the bacteria, taking over the job of the white blood cells. Because Eden took the prescribed antibiotic, her white blood cells didn't get to do their job. The job of her white blood cells is to get rid of the disease-causing bacteria and to build memory cells so those white blood cells can remember to fight off further infections of the same type. The building of the memory cells is called "natural immunity," and it is needed in order for Eden's body to stay strong.

When we were faced with the second ear infection within a month, I decided to try to let Eden's body heal itself. As Eden came to me and told me her ear hurt, the first thing we would do is pray.

I would have her lie down on the same side as the ear that hurt, and she would watch a video, or we would talk. Within half an hour after lying on her ear, she would feel better and get up to play. I increased her dosage of vitamin C and acidophilus, which is a sweet-tasting friendly bacteria in tablet form. Vitamin C and children's acidophilus are totally natural and may be found in a health food store. I took Eden off all dairy products (they produce mucus) and tried to get her to drink a lot of juice.

Once, right at bedtime, she was crying because it hurt her. I prayed over her, lay beside her on her bed and held her close. I thought, *Lord, if she doesn't go right to sleep, I'm going for the medicine.* Well, she did go right to sleep and slept through the night.

It took about two weeks before the whole thing had run its course. The last few days she only mentioned her ear two or three times and then went off to play.

We had won a major victory—Eden's body met the challenge and healed itself. However, within two weeks another ear infection was underway! This time we did the same thing and let her body fight the infection for her. The recovery of the second was about the same time span.

When the third one attacked, she was over it within three days, never once crying and only mentioning it a few times each day. Seven months later, she still hasn't had an ear infection. Of course, I was ready to take her to the medical doctor if the condition worsened. We were glad it didn't, and her body was given the opportunity to do what God created it to do—fight infection.

I'm only sharing here what has worked for us, hopefully to

benefit those who are struggling with sickness in their household. If your healing plan is working for you, you may want to stick with it. Just make the Creator your top consultant!

Health Resources for Parents

For those times when Scott and I are stumped over a recurring symptom in one of our children, we look in a medical reference book, *The Focus on the Family Complete Book on Baby and Child Care*.[1] The book was compiled by Focus on the Family's Physicians Resource Council. It offers detailed definitions and descriptions of common childhood illnesses that help parents evaluate when it's time to contact their child's physician.

It's also a good idea to keep a good book on nutrition on hand. One that my husband and I use is *Prescription for Nutritional Healing* by James and Phyllis Balch.[2] It's not a Christian book, but it contains a lot of wisdom that renews the mind to the nutritional, healing foods and herbs God put in the ground when he decided to make people.

And don't forget the book with the warranties—prayer and the Word of God are always the first place to run to when our child needs healing.

> Beloved, I pray that you may prosper in all things and be in health, just as your soul prospers.
>
> —3 John 2

Father God, in Jesus' name I pray…

Describe one or two of the times when you had a health crisis with one of your children and needed healing for that child. What pathway to healing did you take?

Take a few minutes and look up the following verses about healing. Beside each reference, write the promise God gives about healing in that verse.

- Proverbs 3:7–8
- Proverbs 4:20–22
- Isaiah 53:5
- James 5:14–15
- Exodus 15:26

Preparing for School

13

When my babies were born, I held them up in front of me and watched their legs kick into the air, trying to imagine little lunch boxes in their hands as they skipped out the door to school. I don't know about you, but I loathe the very thought of sending my child into school five days a week for seven hours a day. Yes, I'm the one who just talked about "growing with your child," but letting them go out the door and trusting someone else to train them for that much time every day are scary.

A question every parent of a preschooler has to face is: "When is my child ready to start kindergarten?"

Kindergarten Readiness

The age debate over when a child is ready to go to school is practically as old as school itself. Although the cutoff for the birth date fluctuates from state to state, most schools in the United States allow a child who is five by September 1 to attend kindergarten that year.

I know one school administrator whose son turned five in September and was allowed by state regulation to enter kindergarten that year. She had seen many students enter kindergarten prematurely, and she wanted to be objective with her decision about sending her own son.

This administrator and school principal felt that, although she knew her son would excel academically if he entered school right away, he just wasn't mature enough to handle the other demands of kindergarten life. She held him back for one year so that he started kindergarten just before he turned six the next year. She never regretted her decision.

There is a growing trend to send children to preschool in an effort to gain high academic skills before kindergarten. Kindergarten is not a race. It's the starting point for the love for learning. It's not as much academic as to gain the love of learning. The social skills and learning experiences gained by children in kindergarten will carry on throughout the rest of their school years.

When I took Eden for her three-year checkup, the doctor gave her a pen and paper to see if she could draw a complete circle. A similar type of test is used by some school districts before a child enters kindergarten. Some of the child's capabilities can be traced to his or her perception of what a person looks like. Some educators conclude that if a child draws a person with a circle head and four lines to show arms and legs, they may not be ready for kindergarten. A child who draws a person with arms, face, fingers, toes, eyes, body and other features may be more ready to step into the social, emotional and academic demands of kindergarten life.

Now, before you pull out the pencil and paper, be aware that this is not the only test given for kindergarten academic readiness. There are perceptual skills, shape and name recognition, and other areas of developmental importance. I think that we, the parents, know our children better than anyone else. We will know in our hearts when he or she is ready for a transition from our heart and home into this new social atmosphere and classroom environment. Keep in mind that if you are home with your preschooler, little transition is necessary if you decide to home school. If both parents work outside the home and your child is already in day care, the transition into kindergarten within that same day-care setting should be relatively simple. You may decide to wait an extra year before admitting your son or daughter to kindergarten. God may direct you to teach your little one at home, which may mean simply building on what you have already taught or beginning an entirely new dimension in your relationship with each other.

Facing School When Your Child Is Adopted

Adopting parents face a few mountains in school preparation that other families don't usually think about. If you read my novel, *Daughter of China*, you know some of the horrors of China's one-child policy.[1] By custom the sons take care of parents in their old age, so everyone wants their one child to be a boy. Many families abandon their baby girls in hopes of having a boy later.

The wife of one couple who adopted two Chinese girls, each adopted separately when they were a little older, told me that both of her girls often face questions from people in church or in a department store where they are shopping. When the subject of abandonment comes up, it is difficult for their daughters to know how to respond (or if they must respond at all). The parents were concerned about how the girls would respond to probing personal questions from adults and classmates in school if they were met with a similar line of questioning when Mom and Dad weren't there to help them verbalize their answers.

To overcome this difficulty, the mother read the book *Mommy Far, Mommy Near*, an adoption story, to her adopted girls as a preface to their discussions about their own abandonment stories.[2] She also interacts with them to teach them how to respond to questions. Here is a sample of what this interaction involves, according to the mother:

> I ask her, "Faith, how many mommies do you have?"
>
> "Two mommies," she answers. "My first mommy is a China mommy. The China mommy needed help, so she put me in the police station."
>
> Then I ask my second daughter, who was adopted after she had been in extended foster care, "Elizabeth, how many mommies do you have?"
>
> Elizabeth answers, "I have three mommies. My birth mommy gave me life. My foster mommy loved and helped me. You are my forever American mommy in my forever family."

> "What did your American mommy and daddy promise?" I ask.
>
> "To take care of me forever," my daughter replies.
>
> "Can anybody ever take you away?"
>
> "No. We have paperwork, and we put our hand on a red seal (her handprint and fingerprint on legal adoption documents)."

This mother told me:

> I always ask the girls' permission before I share their stories because it's *their story*. I don't want them to feel ashamed. Arming them with the truth shows them that adoption isn't a badge of shame; it's a banner of love. Their adoption is a picture of our adoption into God's family.

WHAT ABOUT LEARNING DISABILITIES?

Thankfully, the last ten years have seen dramatic increases in knowledge about learning disabilities. New medical research and better diagnostic testing have brought more understanding and acceptance to children who show the physical and emotional implications of being learning disabled.

If you think that your child is showing signs of being learning disabled, and you want to know for sure, you can start by asking their preschool or Sunday school teacher. Some learning-disabled children are perceived as lazy or unwilling to do their work. Or it may seem that they do not pay attention in class. Even worse, some learning-disabled children misbehave in a classroom setting, disrupting other children who are trying to learn. No parent wants to feel that his or her child is problematic for the teacher or for the kindergarten classroom.

Be sure to document any correspondences with teachers or others and present that to a professional learning disability (LD) counselor or your child's pediatrician. For additional information on learning disabilities, you can log on to www.ldonline.org www.ldanatl.org or www.wrightslaw.com.

Which School?

After you know your child is ready for kindergarten, there remains the sometimes difficult decision of which educational system will better serve your child.

Should you home school? How does a person do that? Should you pay for an education at a Christian school? What about public school? If you're like me, you've heard Christian speakers and publications warn against public school, but you have to wonder—can kindergarten or first grade be *that* bad in public school?

There are no pat answers, and I truly believe that every family must hear from God themselves in making this decision. I also believe it's one of the most important decisions you will ever make for your child. God knows what is inside your child better than you do. He has been using all those Bible stories and memory verses and songs you have been teaching your child to build to a big crescendo! He is the supreme advisor on schooling your (His) child.

Making the Decision

When Johnathan was ready for kindergarten, I was blessed to have a Christian school to send my children to. I taught first and second grades in that school before coming home to have my babies, so I knew exactly what they taught and what the strengths and weaknesses were in that school system. More importantly, the teachers there had become my best friends, and I felt more than comfortable sending my son to this Christian school.

Even so, the decision about where he should learn was huge, and we knew we shouldn't base our decision entirely on my own experience or reasoning. Second Corinthians 10:5 tells us that we should, "Refute arguments and theories and reasonings and every proud and lofty thing that sets itself up against the [true] knowledge of God; and we lead every thought and purpose away captive into the obedience of Christ" (AMP).

In quoting this verse, I'm suggesting that gathering facts and information about schools and teachers is important, but ultimately we have to ask God the million-dollar question—"Where do You want my child to attend school?" Experience, fact gathering and counsel are great, but none of these should be held in higher esteem than hearing God tell us what to do concerning schooling our children.

I know some parents who pray every year about each child's education, fully trusting God to speak to their hearts and show them which school to enroll their children in. I've talked to other parents who have settled this question in their hearts forever! They just know that their child belongs in this school or that, or is home schooled every year. It's a decision they came to early on and never looked back.

> He shall feed his flock like a shepherd: he shall gather the lambs with his arm, and carry them in his bosom, and shall gently lead those that are with young.
>
> —ISAIAH 40:11, KJV

God tenderly cares for families (sheep) who have young ones to take care of.

In the tenth chapter of John, Jesus said that His sheep hear His voice, and they do not follow the voice of any other. We can believe that God will speak to us and make His will known to us.

Relying on God is a good place to be—*really!*

THE IDEAL SCHOOL PROMOTES YOUR VALUES

One family from Illinois recently moved from a middle-class neighborhood into a higher-income neighborhood. They made the decision for a lot of good reasons, never guessing the impact it would have on the education of their second grader, Katie.

Katie's second grade class at her new school started every morning with a happy thought. Whenever her mother asked her what her happy thought had been for that day, Katie always replied that she didn't have any happy thoughts to share with her class that day. Katie's mother thought that perhaps her daughter reacted this way because she is a shy little girl.

One day the mother was in her daughter's class when the students started giving their happy thoughts for the day. Katie's mother describes what took place that day:

> The happy thoughts turned to the students' plans for spring break. It went around the room with Brittany who was going to Peru, Carmen who was going to Germany, Brock who was going on a Disney cruise and Andrew who was going to Key West (for the third time this year). Then it was my daughter's turn. I held my breath and wondered if she would tell of her spring break plans (she did have some), but she passed. My heart broke. At the young age of eight she was fully aware that her plans were not on the same scale as the other children's. As I watched my daughter struggle, I wondered if we had made the right decision. We so want our children to grow up knowing the values of life as taught by the Lord, and we want them to know that money doesn't buy happiness.

Prayerfully, Katie's parents made the following wise decisions in this case:

1. The bus stop seemed to be a place of gossip about who has what, so Katie's mom opted to drive her to school.
2. Katie's parents encouraged her friendships with children whose family's values were similar to theirs.
3. They are getting Katie involved in some inner-city service projects so she can see children who have less than she does.
4. They are teaching her practical lessons in money management. For example, she can decide whether she would like one pair of jeans from Limited Too ...or two pairs of jeans from Target.

I want to emphasize here that this situation can happen in any multiple-family classroom setting. Private schools, such as Christian, Catholic, Montessori and classical schools, are usually highly populated by children from high-income families. The average middle-class family has difficulty paying the expenses of private education, especially if they have more than one child. Interestingly, Katie attended a public school that happened to be situated within a higher-income neighborhood.

THE MOST CRITICAL YEAR

Dr. James Dobson, author of numerous best-selling books and founder of the Focus on the Family organization, was asked by a reader in his *Focus on the Family* magazine, "What is the most important period in the spiritual training of children?" I would like to share his answer here:

> Each is important, but I believe the fifth year is often the most critical. Up to that time, a child believes in God because his or her parents say it is the right thing to do. She accepts the reality of Christ as she would a story about Santa Claus or the Easter Bunny—uncritically and innocently.
>
> At about five or six years of age, however, she begins to think more about what she is told. Some kids come to a fork in the road about that time. Either they begin to internalize what they've been taught and make it their own, or else the Bible stories become like fables.
>
> ...I am convinced that our most diligent efforts within the family and our best teachers in Sunday school ought to be assigned to the child of five or six years. There will be crucial crossroads after that, but this one is vital.[3]

After reading that I asked, "OK, this fifth year is crucial... vital...the most important one in their lives. Who is the most spiritually qualified person to teach my child?"

Although I can't answer that question for you, the next chapter is laid out specifically to show an objective point of view on six of the most popular styles of education today—the Christian,

Catholic, classical, Montessori, public and home school educational choices. Please read the following styles of education, paying close attention to the testimonies of parents whose children are being taught within these educational choices and, even more importantly, what God is saying to you as you read.

My friends and I sometimes send e-mail prayers to each other. I know this isn't exactly an e-mail, but right now I want to pray for you.

Father, in the name of Jesus I ask that You will help this father or mother to hear Your voice as he or she reads the next chapter. I fully believe Your promise to "gently lead those that are with young." Lord, You love their child more than anyone else. Please lead them to the right school with the most dynamic undershepherd, one who holds similar values and can lead the child forward during this most important period in their spiritual training. I ask that You will bring agreement between parents or guardians concerning the school choice so that they can approach their child's schooling as a team. I ask for Your peace to be the umpire of their souls now and that they will make no decisions without the complete peace of God ruling their hearts and minds. In Jesus' name, amen.

Happy is the man who finds wisdom,
And the man who gains understanding...
She is a tree of life to those who take hold of her,
And happy are all who retain her.

—Proverbs 3:13, 18

Father God, in Jesus' name I pray…

To help prepare for the next chapter, take a moment to write down some of the spiritual, social, educational and/or personal goals you would like to see accomplished during your child's first year of kindergarten.

After reading this chapter, what are some questions you have about the right choice for your child's education?

Choosing a School

14

By way of introduction, let me just say that I have extensively interviewed educators and parents in order to try to present all of these styles of education in a very positive, objective way. I did not include the specific expenses incurred for each school choice because that varies depending on your location. If one school choice does not seem as complete as it needs to be, please research it further and tell us what you found by logging on to our website at www.charismalife.com. Let us all benefit from your findings!

Let me say a word about homework that will probably get me in trouble with about half the schools on this list. Homework should not rule your home at night. Five minutes (on occasion, ten minutes) of *pencil* homework per grade per night is a good workload scale to go by. For example, the first grader should have no more than five minutes of homework a night. Fifteen minutes is a fair amount for a third grader, and so on. This homework scale does not include reading for pleasure. A good teacher and parent will give ample time for their children to read or be read to on a regular basis, preferably every day.

If a teacher is using time wisely in the classroom, five minutes of pencil-pushing homework per grade should be sufficient time for seatwork and study. Children who are overloaded on homework will often begin to resent reading. Reading a library book becomes a chore instead of a joy. This can be a warning sign that the love of learning is dwindling in your child, and he needs to be rescued from homework overload.

Of course, this homework scale excludes special unit studies where a project is required to be worked on over a period of time. Children, especially the little ones, need time to enjoy warm baths, soft grass, three wheelers and wrestling on the floor.

Remember that you are the parent, and you do not need simply to do whatever your child's teacher or school tells you to do. Sometimes all it takes is for one or two parents to speak up (in a respectful and honoring way) to change an extreme homework load. And give the teacher the benefit of the doubt. A teacher who is relatively new on the job may not realize that the homework load is too heavy. Love believes the best, so approach this issue with love and concern, not suspicion or judgment.

THE CHRISTIAN SCHOOL CHOICE

Most Christian schools follow the same sort of classroom setup and schedule as a public school, complete with music, art, physical education, the basic subjects and recesses. Most Christian schools still use phonics to teach reading. One of several differences is that you are guaranteed that your child's teacher is a Christian, and she will most likely start and end the day with prayer.

A week in Christian school includes Bible class, usually a general assembly, sometimes called *chapel*, and integrates biblical morals, values and character development into the standard curriculum. The standard curriculum, which varies from school to school, usually includes biblical background text and illustrations to most subject matter.

The admissions requirements, discipline guidelines and curricula of Christian schools vary nearly as much as Protestant churches vary. Most Christian schools require at least one of the child's parents to be an active member of a church and require the parent to turn into the school a form signed by their pastor that states they are an active Christian in that church. Some Christian schools add, "An active tithing member of this local church, ______________________ (name of church)."

The majority of Christian schools also use corporal punishment (spanking) as a form of discipline if a student is defiant. It's important that both parents come to terms with allowing someone else to spank your child. I know the people to whom I entrusted my son in kindergarten. I trust their judgment, and I know their heart. I don't think I would have been able to be so free as to allow another person to paddle my child if I didn't know them as well.

Surprisingly, I've known some Christian schools that will still allow students to attend even if the parent objects to corporal punishment. Sometimes the parent and administration can agree upon an alternative discipline route. Don't be afraid to ask questions! Parents sometimes feel shy around teachers and principals in a school. These feelings may stem back to your own school experience of having to submit to everything a teacher or principal says or does. But you are the adult now, and it's vital that you remain on your child's side and on the Lord's side as you seek God's choice for your child's education. This is your child, and you are the one ultimately responsible for his care.

I know that the teachers in the Christian school where I send Johnathan often stop in the middle of the day to pray about a concern or turn on worship tapes during art class and inside recesses.

After a Christian school was started in her church, one mother told me that she and her husband began praying about the school to which they would send their five-year-old. His older sister went to public school and was in the sixth grade.

Different people hear from God in different ways. As this couple prayed, the dad said that everything around him kept pointing to sending his children to a Christian school. Radio shows, conversations with friends and even the desire of the children all seemed to point toward sending them to a Christian school.

For this couple, the biggest obstacle was cost. This couple told me:

> We didn't have any income to send them, but when we prayed, God made provision for it. We took the step of faith, and through the years we were never in a position where we couldn't pay for it. We trusted God, and we even gave a little over what we were supposed to because we believed in what that school was about.

I found my interview with this Christian school family interesting because their oldest child started out in the public school system.

When I asked the mother if there was a difference between her oldest child's kindergarten and first grade experience, and her youngest child's K–1 experience, she said:

> At (my oldest child's) public school, we didn't know the families of her classmates, and she wasn't taught our values. With the Christian school, there was an ongoing relationship with families. I knew them, and we'd watch out for each other's kids. If something was going on in school with our kids' behavior, we'd talk about it and warn each other what to look for to help our child. The biggest advantage is that I knew that the Christian school believed like we did, and the teachers were reinforcing the way we were training up our children.

Another couple, a youth pastor and his wife, added:

> We picked a Christian school because we wanted them to have a Christian background when they're young and impressionable. We wanted a school that would reinforce what we're saying at home.

When I asked this couple about any setbacks in Christian education for the young child, they replied:

> In Christian school, the standards of individual families cover a wide spectrum. They get opinions from other kids. You have a child who is allowed to see this movie or that one, and you feel it's not age appropriate for your child. The differences aren't as drastic as in a public school, but they're still there. They still pick up on attitudes. You have to keep reinforcing your own personal standards and stick to them. For example, our kids always had an earlier bedtime than all the other kids, and they let us know about it.

My sisters and I send our children to three separate Christian schools. My son's school does not tend to overload students with homework. My sisters' children often come home with their arms loaded with books. Consider discussing homework load before you register your child in a school. Each school is different, and most are more than willing to listen to how homework impacts their students' home life.

The Catholic School

Before introducing the Catholic school education, I wanted to be sure to point out that some private schools are geographically kept within set school districts. I spoke to one mother who said her family moved to a new home only to discover they were not permitted to send their child to a Catholic school of her choosing. It was devastating for their family, and, because they had already bought their new home, they felt "pushed" into sending their son to a public school.

For example, in the Philadelphia area, Catholic schools are very strict about geographical boundaries. In south central Pennsylvania, several Catholic schools bus children from eleven different school districts to their school.

Catholic schools focus on a rigorous curriculum that meets or exceeds public school curriculum and includes direct instruction on religion every day. The Catholic school principal that I talked to in my area said that the teachers in her school are quick to pray prayers of thanks when the children are excited about something and quick to pray with them when something sad happens. This principal said:

> For example, on 9/11 we gave the kids words and a tool for what happened. We modeled prayer to show them that this is what you do when you're scared or worried. It's there for the kids. I want them to develop as faith-filled adults and good citizens of this country.

This school's first grade begins with prayers over the public address system, shared prayer, Scripture or the reflection of the day, maybe prayer requests, followed by the flag salute. First graders are expected to complete fifteen minutes of homework each evening in reading and math, and the second half of the year adds spelling to their homework requirements. Some Bible stories are taught to the little ones as nice stories to learn from, but not necessarily as the truth of the Word of God.

The schools generally celebrate major holidays, including "eerie" Halloween parties.

Catholic schools teach all faith traditions and their impact on history, but emphasize what they believe to be "the saints" particular to their Catholic church. For example, St. Joseph's school will study the life and teachings of St. Joseph. The principal that I talked to feels that the Catholic school is a faith community, and the children are surrounded with adults who know them, love them and pray for them.

They use phonics to teach reading, and they test the children each year to be sure the individual child and the classroom are up to national standards of education.

While the education of Catholic schools is up to par, the religious message differs greatly from that of a Protestant Christian school.

THE CLASSICAL EDUCATION—THE STAGES

Classical education may or may not be a new term to you, but classical education has increased in popularity in recent years. Classical education is usually considerably more expensive than Christian school tuition.

Classical education differs from most educational philosophies in that it steps back into the past and attempts to use the tools of learning from yesteryear.

In her well-known essay titled "The Lost Tools of Learning," Dorothy Sayers provides some overview of this medieval model of education.[1] Sayers states that classical education is composed of two parts: the *trivium* and the *quadrivium*.

Classical education believes that young children possess a great natural ability to memorize large amounts of material even though they may not understand its significance. Classical educators drill and fill the minds of five- to eight-year-olds with facts, such as the multiplication table, geography, dates, events, plant and animal classifications—anything that lends itself to easy repetition and assimilation by the mind.

It's not all drill work, though. For example, one mother told me that her second grader's class learned Egyptian history. The teacher set up boxes of about equal sizes on one side of the cafeteria. Using duct tape, they taped off the Nile River. The children had to "quarry the stones" (boxes) and lug them to the edge of the Nile River. Then they piled the stones onto the boat to take it across the river to a waiting "cart," which would drag the "stones" to another section of the cafeteria where the children would build their pyramid.

After the facts are assimilated, the nine- to eleven-year-old child will enter the trivium stage, which, according to Sayers, contains three areas—grammar, dialectic and rhetoric. Each of these three areas is specifically suited to the stages in a child's mental development.

The quadrivium stage involves specialization in particular areas of study, leaning toward the student's particular bent toward mathematics, science, literature or humanities. This stage encourages the students to pursue the area of their natural abilities.

Classical education for the five- to six-year-old

The question is, How would the kindergarten and first grade student learn under the classical approach to education?

One mother in Florida told me she stumbled onto the classical schools while searching for a smaller school for her daughter. "My daughter needed a smaller environment," she told me. "She had a brain tumor and medical problems, and she just needed more personal attention than what she was getting in public school."

Because the textbooks in the classical system were so vastly different from what her daughter was used to, this mother put her child in a small Christian school. But she and her husband were intrigued with classical education and finally decided to educate their younger children through it.

This mother told me:

> The classical approach is my favorite. They do a lot of phonics and writing. My daughter (who is now in first grade) came out of kindergarten knowing both how to spell *autobiography* and how to write one. At the end of grade school, my child will have a stack of bound books she's written. Of course, different children write on different levels. Her class recited all of Psalm 95 at the end of the year, and she knew Mozart.

Her first grader reads fifteen minutes a night in addition to five to fifteen minutes of other homework. The children learn history from kindergarten through twelfth grade, each year using a timeline to build onto the knowledge of history they've accumulated in previous years. Each child also receives his own set of history cards to keep for future reference.

By the time her child reaches fourth grade, she will study Latin, spelling, math and history. She will work on about half an hour of homework each night plus fifteen minutes of reading.

This is a brief overview, but I wanted to provide insight into the classical approach to education from a parent who sent a kindergartner/first grader into this school system.

MONTESSORI SCHOOL

Dr. Maria Montessori initiated the first Montessori classroom in 1907. Today there are thousands of Montessori schools around the world. The Montessori school recognizes and accepts students of any racial, religious, political or social environment. On a broader level, Dr. Montessori sought to cooperate with other organizations to develop education, human rights and peace.

Her approach to education was based on the belief that children should be permitted to progress at their own pace. In her book *The Secret of Childhood*, Dr. Montessori writes, "In the special environment prepared...in our schools, the children themselves found a sentence that expresses the inner need: 'Help me to do it by myself!'"[2]

If your child is already five years of age, she may be too old to begin in a Montessori classroom! The traditional Montessori school will introduce a child into the classroom when the child is two to two and one-half years of age. Montessori schools are not set up with grade level divisions for K–12. Each classroom is designed for a mixing of the age groups—one class has children ages two to six, another ages six to twelve, and still another twelve to fifteen. The child normally starts with a visit to the school followed by a one-hour visit with her teacher a week later. The children are not classified by their age but according to their ability. You can be a three-year-old doing the skill level of a five-year-old. The teacher is trained to recognize the individual child's capabilities and natural abilities and presents a certain level of challenge before that individual child.

According to the Association Montessori Internationale (AMI), the role of a Montessori teacher is that of an observer whose ultimate goal is to intervene less and less as the child develops. Elementary students are taught geography, biology, history, language, mathematics, science, music and art. Children are invited to "explore" each area through field trips outside the classroom to places such as the library, planetarium, botanical garden, science center, factory, hospital and so on.

While spanking a child is practiced in some public schools and most private schools, Montessori teachers do not even tell a child to be quiet. Using the children around them as models, they point to positive behavior and try to reinforce this role modeling so that the child will think it is his idea to work quietly.

While some have found this approach too liberal, others have found it an oasis of learning.

I have a friend whose child is mentally and physically handicapped. She and her husband have found the Montessori school to be of great assistance to them in schooling their challenged child. It was amazing what he was able to learn. His teacher made him a special platform so that his moveable alphabet was on an elevated stand so he wouldn't have to bend over. He was so proud of that personally made stand! He actually learned his letter sounds with the personal attention from this teacher.

There is no homework required of children in the two to six years of age class of Montessori. Children in the upper classes have homework only if they choose to do it. The objective of Montessori is to get the child to make wise choices and work with discipline and skill, so most children actually do choose to do homework.

As with most Christian schools, the Montessori schools in the United States vary, and, as with any school, they are only as good as the teachers are.

THE HOME SCHOOL OPTION

Home schooling, in its simplest definition, means to educate your child at home instead of at a private or public school. Home schooling is probably more diverse in teaching methods than any other educational choice because a parent may use any one of the other educational methods or a mixture of all of them in their child's education.

Home schooling is legal in all fifty states, but regulations and requirements differ in each state. If you are considering home schooling, you can get a copy of your state's home schooling laws by contacting the Home School Legal Defense Association at P. O. Box 3000, Purcellville, VA 20134-9000. Their phone number is (540) 338–5600. You can also visit their website at www.hslda.org.

Of course, the first question in a parent's mind is what to teach and when to teach it. I have found that the answer to this question varies from family to family.

I know one home schooling parent who uses only the A Beka teaching curriculum for her children. She likes the way the program is laid out for each subject and finds it easy to follow as her children progress from year to year. This sweet mother starts her home schooling day at the kitchen table at 10 A.M. and ends at 2 or 3 P.M. Her method of teaching is very methodical, and the children know what to expect from one day (and one subject) to the next.

Other parents prefer to mix and match their materials, throwing out workbooks and resorting to unit studies that rely solely on library books, written and oral reports, and tours to museums, parks and other community resources.

I asked a home schooling friend of mine from the Midwest to relate a day in the life of her first grader. Bear in mind that this first grader has an older brother and sister who are also home schooled! I will let my friend tell you her story now:

A first grader's home school day

> Home schooling for us is more than simply educating our children. It is a lifestyle. Our school days have no set beginning or end. Although some home school families like to flow with the public school vacation and holiday schedule, our home school schedule moves through the entire year, with natural breaks occurring throughout for the holidays, vacations and special needs. We have been doing this for ten years now, and we try to address every aspect of our children's development in planning out our days.
>
> We may begin at 7:00 A.M. with a bike ride around the neighborhood as we enjoy a cool autumn morning. On the other hand, we may find ourselves at a public library at 7:00 P.M., listening to a special guest speaker they have brought in, such as Marion Blumenthal Lazan, coauthor of *Four Perfect Pebbles*. A couple of times a year we find ourselves taking three days off to enjoy hosting out-of-town guests who have come to visit us.
>
> In general, math, spelling and language arts are done daily, but history and science every other. We integrate art as often as possible because children love it. My first grader received piano lessons from his sister in high school.

Physical education consists of jumping on the trampoline and riding bikes.

We try to live out the Scripture, "Seek first the kingdom of God" (Matt. 6:33), and consider prayer to be one of the biggest blessings afforded us as a home schooling family. After beginning with prayer, our first grader might work on a particular Bible verse to be memorized. We often treat ourselves to an Internet episode of "Adventures in Odyssey" while peacefully coloring.

Our youngest son learned to read while sitting next to me on the sofa. We used the book *Teach Your Child to Read in 100 Easy Lessons* in kindergarten and continued on with his reading lessons in the same style. With my arm snug around his shoulders and my head bent over his, we read and enjoyed the Pathway Readers together. Reading and being read to took up several hours of his day.

Because I was teaching more than one child, we experienced many wonderful hours together as I read through classics such as *Swiss Family Robinson* and *The Yearling*. I was not only exposing them to great works of literature, but character building was also going on as we discussed what we had read.

Some of our fondest memories have been created while reading aloud great pieces of literature. I remember the time when we read *The Yearling* together. I literally sobbed at the end of the book. My children still laugh when they tell how they were sitting on the edge of their seats begging me to stop crying and finish reading the story to them! I think they were ready to snatch the book out of my hands and read it for themselves! I live in the country, and we sometimes see deer out in the distance or crossing the road in front of us who fondly remind us of Flag.

Continuing with our language arts, we use the program "Spelling Power" by Beverly L. Adams-Gordon. Because of its setup, we were allowed to go along at our own pace and slowly build up our word base. I incorporated handwriting into his spelling and began to encourage writing skills very early. Single paragraph essays were done, often accompanied with illustrations. As corrections to grammar were made, teaching of concepts was taught naturally.

For math, I chose the curriculum from Bob Jones University and never regretted my investment in purchasing a good set of base ten manipulatives. The early grade workbooks are colorful and simple to use and, more importantly, allow a smooth transition to Saxon Math, which we use in the upper grades. When families home school more than one child, there is sometimes a tendency to use as many nonconsumable materials as possible in order to help balance the cost of materials. Our son was very happy having a workbook of his own that he could write in, and he enjoyed the colorful pictures.

For history or social studies, we invested in computer software purchased from Calvert Academy called "A Child's History of the World." It is an interactive program that has reproduced V. M. Hillyer's book by the same title. The program gives a broad overview from the beginning of time through modern history. Because we lean toward a literature-based style of teaching, we also read together books that have made history come alive—books such as those written by Ingri and Edgar D'Aulaire. *Leif the Lucky* was a particular favorite.

First grade science is fun! We focused on observing and studying the world around our son. A typical science lesson may have involved finding a praying mantis outside, making a temporary home for it in a mason jar and sketching it in our "Nature Notebook." We would then perhaps spend some time looking up this treasure in Faith Comstock's *Handbook of Nature Study*. We have also enjoyed the Nature Readers published by Christian Liberty Press and begin those as soon as independent reading allows. We firmly believe that one of the greatest services we can provide our children is to teach them to appreciate and understand God's world.

Home school challenges

Although home schoolers don't have to contend with the stress of "homework," school fund-raisers or daily runs to and from school and school functions, home schooling families do contend with other unique issues.

Young children may longingly watch the yellow school bus drive by and ask when they will get to ride on a bus. Parents may question themselves and face questioning from others concerning their child's socialization.

Our Midwest home school mom says:

> For many years we were active in an organized play day offered by a local home school support group. Not only did our children experience "recess" outdoors with other children in a park with swings, but they were also allowed an opportunity to play team sports—something our boys very much enjoyed. We have tried to meet our challenges with honesty and prayer, and we have found the Lord faithful in providing satisfying answers, as well as leading us toward fulfilling alternatives.

If you are interested in this avenue of education, the following website proves to be comprehensive in answering questions regarding home schooling: www.geocities.com/Athens/8259/index3.

THE PUBLIC SCHOOL CHOICE

I know a dynamic Christian couple in the ministry who sends all three of their boys to public school. I want to let my friend tell you about their school choice in her own words. The rest of this section includes her report on their public school experience:

> Personally for us, we chose to enroll our children in public school for several reasons. We felt that the covering and prayer they received in our home, as well as our commitment to the ministry at our local fellowship, provided the secure haven and foundations necessary for them to succeed in this educational choice. We also have a strong love

for the community in which we live, and we knew this commitment would provide opportunities to become more involved in tangible ways. We wanted to make a difference in our community by living the gospel in its midst. Our hope is that over the years our children have learned the priceless lessons of sharing their faith and experiencing God's strength and power.

In making this decision, we sought God's guidance as to where we should enroll our children. We were selective about which public school system to enter and were pleased to find a small community where the level of commitment from parents and educators alike is high. Overall, our sons have responded well to this move and have benefited from the opportunities this combination of family life and community affords.

This commitment to public school life has not been without its challenges. We have experienced failure and success along the way. At the very least, this undertaking has deepened our prayer lives. Not a morning goes by where we have not sought God's protection and wisdom for how best to cover our sons. We also have taken every opportunity to be involved in their everyday lives in and out of the classroom. We are well acquainted with all of their teachers and friends, and we try constantly to stay abreast of all they may be facing.

Unfortunately, some of what they have been exposed to has, at times, been more than any parent would care for their children to experience. The onslaught in our society to pervert their natural innocence and strip them of their purity is a constant battlefront. We have drilled into them who they truly are in God, constantly reminding them as they leave in the mornings of the champions they are called to be. "Remember who you are!" is an often-heard encouragement in our home.

We have told them from the beginning that at this time in their lives, they are called to be students. Witnessing the love of God will happen naturally as they hold fast to the truths they know and live lives devoid of compromise. As our sons have become teenagers, our resolve has only strengthened, and we have seen some wonderful fruit from our efforts.

Because of the relationships our sons have with their friends, other children are frequent visitors to our home. One of my oldest son's friends has dubbed our family the "love family" as he has observed the support our children receive, support that is so lacking in his own life. We pray with our sons for their friends and remind them that they are to be young men of influence, not those who are easily influenced.

Others have observed that something is working in our home and wonder what it is that we are doing right. Needless to say, such conversations have been wonderful springboards for planting seeds about the love of God.

A few years ago, one of our sons' teachers actually confided in us about her broken heart over being unable to conceive. God gave us the open door to pray for her and her husband that life would come to her womb. Although she still does not profess Christ, her testimony is that her baby is here because of the prayers that we prayed.

Woven through these years, we continue to work hard at listening. We make sure one of us is home when our boys return home after school just so they know we are available. We do not drill them when they come through the door, but rather we wait for those times when they are ready to talk. Whether it is catching a moment on the way to a soccer game or in the late night sharing with them as they drift off to sleep, we always pray to hear what is on their hearts and keep communication lines open.

For us, choosing public school for our children's education is a lifestyle commitment that involves our entire family. The keys we have found are hearing from God what He would have for our children, and then relying on His grace as we walk out the path He has for us. In *The Message,* the prophet Isaiah wrote, "I stand my ground and hope, I and the children God gave me as signs to Israel, warning signs and hope signs" (Isa. 8:17–18). Our prayer is that our family is a sign of hope and demonstration of God's love in a very real way.

First Grade Burnout

Whatever school choice God leads you to make, it's vitally important not to throw your five- to six-year-old into a daily twelve-hour schedule. This is especially true for preschoolers who have had one parent at home with them all day and are now attending a school outside the home. Although most teachers try to make learning fun, school is work. It's a long day of work for a six-year-old. Your little ones will need some "down time" with Mommy and Daddy, and they will probably need more rest than they did during the carefree days of summer.

When my five-year-old approached his sixth birthday, my son's pediatrician, as well as several well-meaning friends and family members, asked, "Are you going to put him into a sports program?"

Immediately, my mind flashed back to when I taught first graders who had trouble staying awake in class. So many children had organized activities every night of the week—piano lessons, swimming, church, Cub Scouts, Brownies or gymnastics.

This myriad of mental pictures enabled me to answer with conviction, "Not yet."

Many parents rush frantically from school to soccer to ballet to hours of homework, hoping to enhance their children's talents and future.

But according to Alvin Rosenfeld, psychiatrist and coauthor of *The Over-Scheduled Child: Avoiding the Hyper-Parenting Trap*, families should weigh the benefits of participation in extracurricular activities against the costs of time, expense and stress to each family member.[3]

Some families make firm rules, such as one sport per child per season, while others make decisions on a case-by-case basis. *The Focus on the Family Complete Book of Baby and Child Care* advises, "Pay attention to your child's response to his extracurricular activities. Is [this activity] enhancing your family's life and providing some cherished memories or sapping the energy and joy from child and parent alike?"[4]

Parents with multiple children involved in numerous activities can feel like full-time chauffeurs. Sometimes a parent can be torn between attending his son's piano recital and his daughter's soccer game. So watch for the signs of family burnout: frustration, complaining, moodiness and withdrawal.

The founder of a Montessori school related the following story:

> We had a wonderful family in our school who had an eight-year-old girl, a very capable child. We got a note one morning that read, "Please excuse Jamie from ______ (a school activity) because our schedule is as follows..." This eight-year-old girl had at least one activity, and on some days two activities, after school Monday through Friday. Later, Jamie's teachers noticed she was daydreaming a lot. They asked me my opinion on what to do.
>
> I invited her to my office and told her that her teachers were concerned about her. She said, "I'm not daydreaming, I'm resting." She was eight.
>
> I said, "Honey, you are resting from what?"
>
> She said, "I talked with my mother about it, and she said, 'No, you can do it.'"
>
> It turned out that Jamie was in gymnastics, and she was so good at it that the gymnastics teacher said she should be in a special group that trains for two and one-half hours. Evidently, she could potentially be a professional gymnast. She told me, "I can't take it. I love gymnastics, but for a child my age that's too much!"
>
> Of course, this teacher was astonished that this little girl was able to verbalize this for herself and told me that it was a shame that the message had to come from the child. He talked with the parents, and they did cut her schedule back to one hour and fifteen minutes instead of two and a half hours. So some changes were made.

I included this story in an attempt to help us look at our children objectively. It's important that we don't drive our children to do things we think they are good at, or perhaps push them to do an activity we wanted to do as a child but never had the opportunity to do. Children still need time with their families at home, especially after they start school. They need to read books with Mom, wrestle on the floor with Dad and kick the ball around the backyard. Even though they are in school, they need time to be creative and free to go into their pretend world of self-invented drama and skits at home.

If you are concerned about too much activity, take it to God in prayer, and talk to your child. Perhaps your child is the one who wants to do a gazillion after-school activities. Let peace be the umpire of your soul and your family. By striving for a healthy balance of faith, family and fun, you will be better able to evaluate whether or not your first grader is burned-out or benefiting from the activities in which he's involved.

Journal Time

> God gave these...youths great ability to learn and they soon mastered all the literature and science of the time... And in all matters requiring information and balanced judgment, the king found these young men's advice ten times better.
>
> —Daniel 1:17, 20, TLB

Father God, in Jesus' name I pray...

Take a moment to read over the goals you wrote down in the last chapter. After reading this chapter on the various school choices available, do you feel that there are one or two school choices that would best fulfill your goals for your child? Which one(s)?

As you read this chapter on choosing the right school, did the Holy Spirit speak a *yes* or *no* to you concerning a particular school choice? Take a moment to jot down what He is showing you.

Prepared for Service 15

As parents, we desperately need God's help in preparing our child for school, don't we? The good news is that God is in your court—He's right there on your side, scoring home runs that you may not even see right away.

I want to share my own personal story of how God prepared me for first grade, that I actually did hear God speak to my heart, and how He used me for His service as a child.

Hearing God at Six Years Old

I never went to kindergarten. My family moved from the Washington, DC, area to northern Pennsylvania that year and, although we had never heard of the term *home school,* that's exactly what my mother did to prepare me for my first grade education.

One summer, just before entering first grade, Dad and I were walking through an orchard where we lived in northern Pennsylvania. We were holding hands and talking. The whole time we talked, the Holy Spirit was speaking to my heart. I can't remember most of what Dad and I talked about that day, but I do remember what the Holy Spirit said! He told me He wanted me to go pray—alone.

I wasn't sure exactly how to go about obeying the Holy Spirit. My parents were in the ministry by then, and the five of us lived in a very small trailer on a Christian campground. It was hard to get alone!

One day, when I felt it was the right time, I knelt by my bunk bed and began to pray.

TAP, TAP, TAP. Someone was at the door. It was my best friend, Amy, whose family also worked and lived at the camp year round.

"Can you come out and play?" she asked.

It was tempting, but I knew I was supposed to pray. "No, I can't," I answered. "I'm praying."

"Praying?" she asked. "But Danny's here and everything, and we're going to play on the log." The old fallen tree was my favorite play spot, and I rarely got to see fun-loving Danny. I was strongly tempted, but I shook my head no.

I don't remember much more, except that I turned down play to pray, and I didn't stop praying until I felt God's hand lift. As I look back on it now, I believe that God filled me with, what D. L. Moody called, "His mighty power from on high."

God was preparing me for first grade by bringing me into complete surrender to Him. Little did I know that when I entered my public school classroom for the first time, God would use me to begin a revival that very day.

CARRYING REVIVAL

I was six years old when my best friend, Amy, and I boarded the bus the first day of school. The bus was nearly empty, so we sat together and sang the Christian songs we had learned from our home, Arrowhead Awana Camp. The bus moved on, collecting new passengers on the way.

Both of us were startled when suddenly the bus exploded with applause and cheers. We looked around to see what was going on. Everyone was looking at us!

Without knowing it, we were singing to a busload of elementary school students—and they asked for more!

"WHO'S JESUS?"

On my first day of first grade, I went into my classroom and found that each of us had modeling clay on our desks. We were told to make something with the modeling clay and talk softly until the teacher came to class.

Without trying to, I talked about Jesus.

A little girl asked me, "Who's Jesus?"

I was absolutely stunned.

"You mean, you don't know who Jesus is?" I asked incredulously.

She shook her head. Boy, did I have a heart full of Bible for her! I told her she could get saved if she wanted to.

"I want to get saved, too!" another girl cried.

I told them to meet me at the bathroom later.

Recess came, and instead of running outside to play, I met with the girls at the bathroom. I wasn't sure how to go about salvation in a bathroom, but I knew how to get saved in a church. So I picked the toilet as the altar and told them to kneel down!

By the end of the second recess, both of those girls gave their hearts to Jesus.

By day two, more of the girls in my class wanted to be saved. I was so delighted to lead them to Jesus. Looking back on it now, I realize that the teachers must have known what was going on and let it happen, because for the next several weeks I spent every recess in the bathroom leading girls to Jesus.

Giving up recess I walked to the bathroom one day and saw a long line of girls standing outside the bathroom, all waiting to come in and pray with me at the toilet. As far as I can remember, the lines formed for several days.

In all that time, I don't remember going outside for one recess. I knew in my heart that God was asking me to sacrifice my playtime and obey Him. Yet I was so happy, even without recess!

One day a boy wanted to get saved. It took some hard thinking on my part to figure out how to get a boy redeemed in the girls' bathroom!

Finally, I knew what to do. I told him to meet me at the big rock just outside the school door, next to the playground.

After that little boy was saved, I looked around me. No one else was waiting to get saved. I looked longingly at the swing sets and playground equipment. I could play! I charged off to the playground, just in time to hear the teacher's whistle to line up.

THE ENEMY COMES IN

What do you think the devil was doing the whole time I was leading children to Jesus? If you guessed, "Trying to figure out a way to shut you up," you're right!

Unlike Silver Lake Elementary, the elementary school I entered in south central Pennsylvania was full of fear, anxiety and hatred. My first grade teacher paddled children all the time. We would line up at her desk to show her our work. If we didn't do a paper correctly, she pulled out her paddle and paddled us right there in front of everyone.

I remember painting one time. She had warned all of us not to get any paint on anything but our hands. I didn't care one lick about what my picture looked like—I just did my best to keep the paint off me. When I went to the back sink to wash, the teacher saw paint on my elbow and slapped me hard and yelled at me. I cringed as the tears slipped out.

I grew to fear rainy days. On rainy days, my teacher came out to the playground with her paddle and grabbed every child who forgot to wear boots to school and paddled them for not being dressed properly. I wanted to wear boots every day to be sure I was prepared. Some of the poorer kids didn't even own boots.

FIRST GRADE NIGHTMARE

My new first grade class was a living nightmare, a total reversal of my life in the Spirit as I knew it. Where I used to be very extroverted and talkative, I became painfully quiet and shy. Later on, my elementary teachers used to write on the back of my report cards, "Cynthia (my first name) talks so softly we can barely hear her. We're working on getting her to speak up."

I began to wish that I was in the other first grade teacher's classroom until one day, when our door was open, I heard the other teacher yelling fiercely at the children in her class, too.

My teacher stood girls on top of their desks, pulled up their dresses in front of everyone and paddled them. I can't remember if I endured this humiliation or not. It was my greatest fear. I was paddled, like everyone else, for not putting my name on a paper or whatever. (She gave me mostly As on my report card.)

I never really knew what I did to cause her wrath. Every time I was paddled, though, I shook with fear and wet my pants. I remember seeing my underwear drying out on the radiator up front several times. She was always nice about drying it out for me. Maybe it made her feel bad, or perhaps she was concerned that my parents would find out. I don't know.

I am going into all of this detail to make a point. First of all, my mother and father had no idea what I was going through every day. They went to several PTA meetings and never once did my teacher tell them that I had been paddled at all. I didn't even tell them about it until I was an adult! Why?

I was trained that authority is always right. I was convinced that, even though I was petrified of my first grade teacher, she was always right. I suffered many nightmares, guilty thoughts and tormenting fear from that class. And I didn't want my parents to be ashamed that I was such a bad girl in school. I was a teenager before I realized I really hadn't been a bad girl at all.

This may come as a surprise to you, but most children lack the ability to communicate their feelings. They know to cry when they are hurt, but to just walk up to an adult and tell that adult some gut-wrenching emotion that is harboring in their soul is rare indeed. Children are concrete thinkers, seeing everything as black and white and no in-betweens. Because I was raised by loving authorities and taught to obey them, I assumed that those in authority over me were always right.

Covering Your Child

I began life in first grade in the Spirit, but my spirit was crushed by the end of that year. From that year until the end of sixth grade, most of my prayers and contemplation about my future were based on fear.

My prayer life took on timid cries of, "Lord, God, please let me have the nice teacher in the next grade instead of that mean one." "Lord, please don't let me do something wrong on this paper." "Lord, help me to be good every day until summer." "Lord, help me not to have bad dreams anymore."

In training your child to follow the things of the Spirit, you will need to be the protector and covering over them. If there is anything of God going on in your home, you can be sure that the devil is working on a plan to stop it. The devil would like nothing more than for every sincere Christian to become so busy with Christian activities that they lose touch with the child they are raising and the God they are serving.

> For our struggle is not against flesh and blood [people], but against the rulers, against the authorities, against the powers of this dark world.
>
> —EPHESIANS 6:12, NIV

There is power in the blood of Jesus. I pray nightly for that powerful blood covenant to rest upon my children, providing peace, security and protection from the schemes of Satan.

THE DEVIL'S PLAN

At six years of age, I didn't know a thing about the devil. My parents' background of teaching didn't provide them with much knowledge about the devil either. But according to biblical accounts, devilish strategies have been used for thousands of years.

For example, the devil possessed the pharaoh of Egypt to kill all baby boys. Moses escaped death through the wisdom and skill of a godly mother. The devil possessed Herod with jealousy until he killed every baby in Bethlehem while seeking to kill the Christ child.

As parents, it is tempting to raise our child in the fear of the unknown instead of faith in God to warn and help us in what lies ahead. If we stay in touch with God, then He who searches hearts, even your child's heart, will reveal to you the mind of the

Spirit in every matter. (See Romans 8:27.)

The greatest parent of all, Father God, has every intention of teaching us how to parent our child successfully. He has commissioned His Spirit to guide us into spiritually preparing our preschoolers.

> For I know the thoughts that I think toward you, says the Lord, thoughts of peace and not of evil, to give you a future and a hope.
>
> —Jeremiah 29:11

Father God, in Jesus' name I pray…

Describe your own early school experience and write down how it positively or negatively impacted your life:

Now describe the school experience you would like your children to have. List the ways you want your children's lives to be impacted *positively* by their school experience:

16 Children Yielded to the Spirit

I was struggling with my same old battle—the temptation to indulge 'til I bulge with foods that are not good for my body. Ouch. It hurts to admit it, but food can be my downfall. Recently I have been striving to gain a taste and appetite for food that is good for me.

I was doing fine for a few weeks until one day, after visiting with my friend, she insisted that I take home a big Ziploc bag full of assorted cookies.

"Oh, no," I cried. "Chocolate chip cookies are in there? Please, they're wonderful but I want you to keep them..."

"Throw them in your freezer," she said.

"I'll pull them out and eat them," I replied.

"Take them home to your kids," she countered.

"They don't eat very much. I'll end up eating them."

"Come on..."

She won. I took them home. I should have walked them straight to our outdoor garbage can, but it seemed an ungrateful thing to do, so I brought them in the house. Big mistake!

A "Holey" Picture

The next morning after I had indulged in at least six chocolate chip cookies, my three-year-old Eden brought me a picture she had made for me.

"What's this, Honey?" I asked.

"That's you, Mommy. You have a hole in your mouth and a hole in your belly button." (Just to emphasize the holes, she poked her pencil straight through the paper at the mouth and belly button.)

I thought, *Who told you?*

"What's all the rest of this stuff?" I asked, pointing to the scribbles of lines all around her little drawing of Mommy.

"You're all tangled up, Mommy," Eden simply replied.

I caught my breath. Never had I seen a truer portrait of myself—big holes in my mouth and belly button and strings tangling me up. I realized God somehow had a hand on my little girl's drawing.

"Eden, I have a question for you."

"What?" she asked.

"How can Mommy get all those tangles off of her?"

"I'll draw you a new picture—one without all the tangles," she said, with a reassuring smile.

At that moment the Holy Spirit spoke to me. I thought that Eden would tell me that she was going to erase the tangles and fix the picture. Through her picture, God showed me that He's able to create me all over again—make a new picture and throw away the old one.

That thought gave me hope the next few days and added strength to my soul that not only could God help me, but also that He had spoken through a three-year-old to tell me that He is watching me and that He cares.

Eden still doesn't know how God spoke to me through her drawing. At three years of age she can't even understand how God used her.

"I Have Been Your Leader From My Youth..."

God does use children in a very real way. If we set them apart from the world and keep Christ before them, they have much greater capacity to be used by God in a pure way.

At the end of his life, Samuel testified to the people, "I have walked before you from my childhood" (1 Sam. 12:2). The New International Version says, "I have been your leader from my youth until this day."

God said to Jeremiah, "Before I formed you in the womb I

knew you; before you were born I sanctified you; I ordained you a prophet to the nations" (Jer. 1:5).

Jeremiah argued, "Ah, Lord GOD! Behold, I cannot speak, for I am a youth" (v. 6).

God answered, "Do not say, 'I am a youth'" (v. 7).

The Word of God also admonishes, "Don't let anyone look down on you because you are young, but set an example for the believers in speech, in life, in love, in faith and in purity" (1 Tim. 4:12, NIV).

GOD USES CHILDREN

Children are wonderfully sensitive to the Holy Spirit. Some adults tend to downplay their significance in the kingdom of God, but God can use a little child to speak into the most secret places of our hearts and thoughts.

In his book *Children Aflame*, David Walters warns Christian parents and those involved in Christian education not to be content with merely raising good children. "We must seek to raise godly, anointed ones that know their God. It is so easy to be content with your children 'having a form of godliness, but denying its power' (2 Tim.3:5)."[1]

In the 1700s, John Wesley was mightily used by God in revivals throughout England, Scotland and the United States. Please allow me to share an excerpt from one of his journal entries:

> 8/6/1784—I came to Stockton-on-Tees. Here I found an uncommon work of God among the children. Many of them from six to fourteen years, were under serious impressions, and earnestly desirous to save their souls... Is this not a new thing in the earth? God begins His work in children. Thus it has also been in Cornwall, Manchester, and Epworth. Thus the flame spreads to those of riper years; till at length they all know Him, and praise Him, from the least unto the greatest.[2]

During the Welsh Revival, at the turn of this century, God

moved mightily upon young children and teenagers who went out into the streets singing and witnessing. Large meetings grew out of their obedience to the Holy Spirit.

Classroom Visions of the Cross

I was teaching first and second graders in our children's church one Sunday evening using wonderful picture cards that depict the way the tabernacle was set up in the Old Testament. We saw how the pieces, if we'd connect them together like dot-to-dot, were in the shape of a cross. The lesson became intense when I showed the holy of holies with the Shekinah glory of God over the mercy seat between the angels. It was awesome to think about the angels in heaven shouting, "Holy, holy, holy." We talked about the Shekinah glory of God, and how we are the temple of the Holy Spirit now, and His glory is *in* us. The children were listening intently, eager to know more.

I said, "Let's lift our hands like the angels of heaven and say, 'Holy, holy, holy,' to God." That was that. God took over. I felt prompted to go to the window.

We all went to the back window to look at the orange and pink sun surrounded by fluorescent pink and brilliant blue.

Because we had just finished talking about the Shekinah glory of God over the mercy seat, I said, "Imagine how beautiful the colors of heaven are, and the glory of God that is there."

One boy, whom I will call David, turned to me and said that he saw the cross of Jesus. "Yeah, I saw it, too," said another, and then another.

Where?" I asked.

"Out there," they all pointed.

All three children saw this bright illuminated cross. The rest of us stood at the large window, our noses pressed against the glass, but did not see it.

I thought, *That's awesome, God. Thanks.*

Each of the three children described the cross in the same way—white, clear, bright rays all around it.

David said, "I see Jesus on the cross with the nails on His hands and feet and the crown on His head and the big stab in His side." The other two excitedly affirmed that they too saw what David saw. The rest of us again pressed our noses to the glass, searching for the cross the others saw.

I didn't know what to make of their vision, but I never tell children that what they are seeing is not real or not from God. I am excited when God shows things to children.

Finally, we all sat down at our desks. The Holy Spirit told me to play a song. I didn't even sing at first. The glory and power of God gently came over the children. I heard one of them weeping.

One little girl was bent forward over her desk, and she said, "There's like a heavy weight on my back, and I can't make my back straight."

I told her that the glory of God sometimes feels like a weight, a good weight, that settles on us.

More children began to cry until most of them were weeping. I wrote some things down as it happened. After I went home, I wrote down some other things exactly as I remembered them. For the most part, I just tried to stay out of God's way as He moved on the children that evening.

As I was playing the keyboard and children were weeping, at one point the Holy Spirit told me to have David come to the front and preach. I waited to be sure that I was hearing God because I know how shy David is. Suddenly, David walked up front by himself, and all I had to do was ask him, "What is God saying to you, David? What do you see?"

I'm about to share with you the precious, sweet vision that little David had. I don't want to change his wording because it gives his innocent perspective. God opened David's eyes to see the death and resurrection of His Son. This story comes alive as it's told from his perspective:

> I saw Jesus at the last supper, Him and His disciples with the bread and wine. Then I saw Judas go away. Then I saw Jesus going over to the Garden of Gethsemane—I think it

is called that—is that right? [I nodded.]

I saw Him pray at the rock, and I saw Him pray and instead of sweat there was blood dripping down like sweat onto the rock. Then I saw an angel come to strengthen Him. It just came over in front of Jesus and shined.

Then I saw the guards come and take Him and I saw Judas betray Him. I saw Jesus get pushed by the guards to get over to the—what's it called? Where the Pharisees lived—they're the ones who betrayed Jesus. They went just outside of the synagogue—what do you call it, where the Pharisees lived? [I shrugged my shoulders. I didn't know.] And outside the guards hit Him and beat Him with their clubs. They held His chin up and hit Him in the face. Then He went in to the Pharisees. I forget what the Pharisees said, though.

After they talked, they took Him outside the city to Pilate, and Pilate had Barabbas and Jesus on both sides of his hands, and they were both chained, and he had people down under his feet, but not like under your feet, but out there. [David pointed out in front of him.]

And the people yelled, "Let Barabbas go, let Barabbas go," and Pilate didn't want to let Barabbas go and make Jesus die, but he did what the people said and washed his hands and made the guards do it.

The guards took him, and one walked up to get his whips and get the crown on. They were still walking. Now they're at the place where they get whipped. They tied his hands to the pole and took a rope or something like that, that had, what's it called, hard like, little balls on the end, and whipped Him.

They took Him off the rope—He was on a rope from the pole—and they took Him over someplace, I don't know. They put the crown on Him. Then they put the robe on Him, a purple robe, and then they mocked Him and bowed down to Him and made fun of Him. Then they took Him up to Calvary. He was carrying the cross. On the way, Jesus was in front, and one of the guards stabbed Him in the side with a spear to get moving.

> Here's when I started to cry harder. I could cry right now. A little while later I saw Jesus, and I started to cry. Then He said, "No use for weeping, for I will come again," something like that. When He said that I felt, you know, His words were like powerful and love, and He had the sweetest voice.
>
> While they were walking, Jesus got tired and fell down [the Holy Spirit spoke to me at this point and said, "He's telling you the TRUTH," and I shivered] and somebody spit on him.
>
> They picked a guy named, I forget his name, Matthew or something, he carried the cross up to Calvary, crying on his way. Tears were coming out of his eyes. Then they got to Calvary and he, Matthew, gave the cross to the soldiers, still weeping while he was doing it. Then they took Jesus and pulled out His beard, and then they took a real hard stick or something and hit Him in the head, the stick was badder than the other clubs, it was real strong. The other clubs were just like little sticks. They hit Him in the head two times. Then they took Him and put Him down on the cross, and then they took a pretty long nail and they hammered it through His wrist. They nailed Him on His feet. They set the cross up.
>
> Next I saw Jesus rising again. I wasn't there—I just saw it. I saw Jesus—it was cool. There was, like, His body was all bright. You could hardly see Him, and then there were rays shining out from His body. He was walking out of the tomb. He folded up all the sheets. The end.

"David, why are you crying?" I asked him softly.

"I started crying because Jesus was so strong on me," he answered. "Tears were getting all over me. The power of God was on me."

Tears "got all over" Latinya, too, as she cried lying on her back on the floor, her arms straight up in the air. "More, more, more, more, more," she cried. "I want more, Jesus, more, more, more, more, more." Over and over she cried out to God for forty-five minutes or more.

I have gone into great detail here to tell you the story of Jesus meeting His children in a classroom. I taught about the tabernacle, the holy of holies, the mercy seat, the blood on the mercy seat, the angels and the Shekinah glory of God. The rest of the time, God took over. This was not the only time God met us, but it was the most recent, and I wanted to share it with you.

Let me stop here for just one more moment. Perhaps you picked up this book hoping to get some pointers on being a good parent. If you have been wondering what being a Christian is really all about, David just told us the true story of Jesus. It's all in the Bible. Perhaps you've read this story with me, and you are weeping, too. The Bible says, "Behold what manner of love the Father has bestowed on us, that we should be called children of God!" (1 John 3:1). God told His Son to go through all of this suffering to pay for our sins so that we could become God's sons and daughters. He raised Jesus up from the dead to show us that He plans to raise all of us from the dead to live forever with Him.

The Bible tells us how to become His child. Romans 10:9 says, "If you confess with your mouth, 'Jesus is Lord', and believe in your heart that God raised him from the dead, you will be saved" (NIV). If you have never believed in Jesus, you can do it now. You can talk to God on your own, or say this prayer from your heart:

> *God, I believe You sent Jesus to die on the cross for me. I've done bad things, and I believe that Jesus paid for my sins when He died on the cross. I believe You raised Jesus from the dead, and I believe You will also save me from eternal death and take my spirit to heaven when I die. In Jesus' name, amen.*

Please, if you have prayed this prayer, contact me through e-mail at my website: www.seehope.com. Or e-mail pray4me@strang.com, and someone will be glad to talk to you about Jesus. And do tell someone, a friend or family member, about your decision to believe in Jesus.

PRAISE THE LORD, HALLELUJAH AND AMEN

During his travels in the United States, David Walters met a small blonde-haired girl three years of age. The girl's mother told Brother Walters, "She is very verbal. She watches Joyce Meyer all the time."

"Oh, yes I watch Joyce Meyer every day," the little girl quickly told him. "And when she finishes preaching I say, 'Praise the Lord, hallelujah and amen.' I'm going to be a preacher."

"I think you already are," replied David, in his English accent. "Do you want to come with me to be a helper?"

"Oh, YES," she replied, ready to go with him to preach.[3]

Another father tells of his four-year-old son who had the television on watching John Hagee.

He said to his son, "I'm going to turn it."

"No, no," he answered. "I don't want to watch cartoons. I want to watch John Hagee preach."

THE SILO WITH A HOUSE ON TOP

A family was driving home from Milwaukee when six-year-old Jordan said, "Mom, I feel like God wants us to stop at a house on the way home."

"Do you know why?" the mother asked wisely.

"I feel like there's someone there who is hurting," Jordan answered.

Wondering how they would know which house to stop at, the mother asked, "What does the house look like?"

"It's the place that has the silo with a house on top," he answered. "It'll be on the right."

Jordan's mom wondered if her son was hallucinating.

Within minutes he said, "It's coming up! It's coming up! It's right up here!"

The highway, which they rarely traveled, was divided and there were no landmarks or signs, only trees and fields everywhere. Within minutes, everyone saw the silo—with a doghouse on top of it. Go figure...

Finding the farm off the exit was one thing, walking up to the front door and offering prayer was quite another. The family sat in their car and prayed, seeking God as to what to do next. Mustering courage, the family walked up to the front door and knocked. A man came to the door. Jordan's mother explained what Jordan had told her and asked the man if there was anyone hurting in that house.

The man looked stunned, then explained that he had been suffering for two years with a severe neck problem and the doctors were unable to help him with the pain. At the very moment the family walked up to the house, the man was on the Internet looking for help!

Jordan's job must have been done, because as his parents prayed for the man, Jordan went off (being a kid) on their swing set. The man was in tears with gratitude.

"I Saw the City"

Johnathan was two and one-half years old when my husband and I were concerned that he was growing too attached to me. We went virtually everywhere together, and when we separated for any reason, Johnathan was quick to let me know he was not pleased with the separation. We frequently encouraged him to be less attached to Mommy.

One evening at the supper table someone mentioned the word *city*.

"I saw the city," Johnathan piped up.

"You did?" I asked.

"I visited Jesus."

"What did Jesus say?" I asked.

"He said to go back to my mommy."

"What else did you see?" I asked.

"The disciples."

We were quiet and waited. Johnathan spoke again.

"Jesus told me that when He was a little boy like me, He

wanted His mommy, too."

"Yes, Jesus was a boy like you at one time," I answered.

As he spoke, I was filled with awe. I also felt as though the Lord had properly corrected me. Johnathan was attached to me, and, at two and one-half years old, that was OK with God!

I have had children tell me that they have seen Jesus, the devil, angels, horses and heaven. Some children have vivid imaginations, and they tell stories from those imaginations. At other times, children really do see things of the heavenly realm, both when they are awake and asleep.

I think, *What if we wouldn't have stopped long enough to listen to Johnathan tell about the city he saw? What if we wouldn't have been quiet and let him get through telling it? What if one of us put him down or even laughed in disbelief when he said he saw Jesus?*

Well, we did listen. More importantly, Johnathan listened because God had something to say to this preschooler—and he has something to say to your preschooler, too!

THE NYPD/FDNY MIRACLE— BEFORE THE TOWERS FELL

I usually like to refer to more updated testimonies, but this one is special because of its location and the testimony it was to New York's policemen (NYPD) and firemen (FDNY).

A friend of mine took her family on a sightseeing tour to the World Trade Center during Easter of 1999, just two years before the towers fell. She and her family were getting on an escalator that was extended about three times the normal length of an escalator. I will let this mother tell you her story:

> As I was helping her older sister who was afraid of escalators, my four-year-old daughter Angela got on in front of me without my help. We were about halfway down, and she looked up at me and said, "OUCH."
>
> "What is the matter?" I asked.
>
> "My foot."
>
> I looked down and saw her foot, and it was being

"eaten" by the escalator. She had on a pair of leather Keds. Later, I found out that she had been tapping the leather molding on the side of the shoe against the side of the escalator where it meets the steps. Her foot went in and began to go down into the escalator.

I yelled out, "Reverse this thing!"

My husband took off running down the front, and my sister's eighteen-year-old son took off running to the top, both running for the automatic emergency shut off.

There were two huge sets of escalators. They were very long from top to bottom. My daughter Angela, who was not crying, pointed to the one going the opposite direction and said, "There's an angel."

Before anybody got to any of the escalator switches, everything stopped. The other escalator kept going, but ours stopped before anyone got there to turn it off.

The NYPD and FDNY came out of the woodwork. One of the firemen saw the condition of her foot and asked her if it hurt.

Angela told them, "It hurt at first, but it doesn't hurt anymore."

It had been about two minutes since her foot was first caught.

I looked in Angela's eyes, and I saw that she was looking to me. Her hand was shaking a little, and her eyes were wide like she was going into shock. I called to the Holy Spirit that I needed Him, and I was suddenly able to push out of my mind everything that was happening, and I spoke peace over her.

I said, "Everything will be all right, Honey. God is in control. No weapon formed against us will prosper. God is with us right now; even in this situation the peace of God is holding us."

She looked in my eyes and asked, "Will I walk again?"

I thought, *I can't answer something I don't know for sure.*

I asked under my breath, "Father?"

He answered, "Yes."

I told her, "Yes, you will walk again. No weapon formed against us will prosper."

She repeated this, and I kept soothing her with the peace of God. He tried to calm her, and I was the channel He used to bring peace.

It took about twelve minutes. They had to take the steps apart and cut the shoe off from the back because part of her shoe had been eaten. They took off the metal until they could easily lift her foot out of there. Her foot was the depth of a piece of notebook paper, and there was quite a bit of blood on the bottom of her foot.

My sister said, "Honey, I want you to know that reconstructive surgery is not a big deal. They can reconstruct a foot. Because of her age, and how the bones are, it will be easier to do reconstructive surgery on her than anybody that's older."

A lot of skin was peeled back on the bottom of the foot. Angela always had a difficult time with blood, but she never saw the blood. She couldn't see the bottom of her foot. The nerves were damaged, and she didn't have the ability to turn her foot and look at the bottom of it. I was so thankful that she couldn't see it.

While in the ambulance, the paramedic told Angela, "You know, when I was a little boy, my foot was crushed in an escalator."

She looked out over the gurney at his foot and saw it was whole.

Then she looked up at me, and I said, "See, his foot was healed."

She said, "Yes, Mommy!"

Right after that, she yelled, "OUCH!"

Everyone jumped to see what happened.

The paramedics lifted the sheet, and her foot was back to its normal size, no swelling, no bruises and no more bleeding.

I believe she suddenly had faith to believe. She looked at me, but she made the decision. Jesus said, "Your faith has made you whole; go." She looked at his foot and saw he was walking, and it gave her faith to believe.

The hospital x-rays showed no damage at all. There was

no fissure, fracture, bone damage, nothing.

I told one fireman, "This is a witness to the power of God."

The pediatrician scratched her head and said, "She's obviously one of the lucky ones. There's not a fracture or fissure, nothing broken, shattered or even a blood vessel split. I don't know what happened. She's obviously lucky."

I said, "Well, we know what happened; we've been crying out to God."

Angela told the doctor, "I will walk again."

The doctor said, "I don't want you to walk for a couple of days. It'll be so sore you won't want to walk. When you want to walk, you can go ahead and walk again."

That very night as her mother got up to get her a snack out of a vending machine, Angela got up because she wanted to pick out what she wanted to eat. She walked over to the machine to make her choice and has been walking ever since. She didn't need the two days of ibuprofen that the doctor said she'd need, and she experienced no swelling, pain or bruising.

My sister works in an emergency room in Texas, and she told us, "I've seen a lot of trauma come through. This is miraculous."

Angela tells everyone about her miracle. Our older daughters who watched it all believe God so much stronger than before. It affected our walk, our talk, even the way we believe. God is awesome!

The Holy Spirit Speaks to Adopted Children

There is a precious little four-year-old girl named Ruth who was brought to her forever home from China when she was ten months old. Ruth's parents were considering adopting a little girl named Faith from Vietnam, but they were careful not to discuss their thoughts with Ruth until they knew for sure that God was calling them to adopt again.

One morning Ruth and her parents were sitting at their family breakfast nook, talking about pretty names for girls when

Ruth asked her mother, "What are we going to name the baby?"

Jokingly, her mother replied, "Jessica is a pretty name."

"No," Ruth emphatically stated. "The baby's name is Faith. Jessica is in China. Faith is in Vietnam."

Faith was indeed born in Vietnam with numerous physical abnormalities, including congenital scoliosis and a very shortened left arm. Her heart is located on the right side of her chest, and at four months of age, she was taken to a hospital with bronchitis, which turned into pneumonia. Several times during her lengthy hospitalization her doctors didn't expect her to make it through the night.

Faith not only made it through the night, but she also made it to her forever family in America, just as Ruth predicted. Faith's orphanage caretakers told her American mother that Faith was very strong—other babies who were as sick as she was had died.

After she had been with her Christian American family for about one and one-half years, when she was only two and one-half years old, Faith saw some unusual things when her mother tucked her in at bedtime. Let's hear this story in the mother's own words:

> As I prayed with Faith, her attention was drawn away from me. I asked her if there were angels in the room, and she promptly pointed out one over her crib. You should have seen the smile on her face and the twinkling in her eyes. She then pointed out another one, smiling just as broadly. I continued praying and was interrupted again. She pointed out another angel near the door to the room. I stopped praying and told Faith that I wished I could see angels and said maybe I should pray that God will let me see them. She nodded and said, "Yeah!"
>
> We finished praying, said goodnight and kissed. Aloud, Faith said that she *is* healed and thanked Jesus, and then said goodnight. Then she looked toward the angels and told them, "I love you!"
>
> Baby Faith is now three years old, living with her big sister Ruth and her family. She loves to worship Jesus by

> waving a little handmade streamer or flag (just her size) in church. Sometimes, when she can't find that flag at home, she'll wave a burp cloth or a dust cloth in the air to praise Jesus!

And Jessica? Her story is yet to be written!

Life in the Spirit

Life in the Spirit is exciting! God is real, heaven is real, and angels are real. Why shouldn't we experience the kingdom of heaven on earth? Jesus told us to pray that God's will would be done on earth as it is in heaven. God can reveal heaven to us just as He did to Paul and John in the revelations He gave them, or as He revealed the kingdom of heaven to Peter, James and John when He was transfigured before them and talked with two of heaven's citizens, Elijah and Moses.

Just a word of wisdom here—I don't think that it is wise to lay aside normal preschool life for a few years and hide out in a cabin somewhere to seek supernatural experiences for ourselves or for our children. (Although it does sound like a fun way to spend a weekend!)

God is the boss. And He loves faith. Can I tell you that God is so very drawn to faith that it just makes Him smile all over us when we have it? As a family, we tell God aloud that we want Him to show up in our home and to be in our dreams and in our times of praise. We don't want to ruin His movements in our family by being doubtful or afraid of supernatural things when they happen. All good gifts come from the Father.

Children's thoughts and desires aren't nearly so cluttered and demanded upon as adults. We must not underestimate our children's spiritual and mental capabilities. The Holy Spirit is just as big inside a three-year-old as He is inside that child's parents. God loves to reveal the thoughts of His heart to big or little people who are sensitive enough to listen.

Journal Time

> For this reason I bow my knees to the Father of our Lord Jesus Christ, from whom the whole family in heaven and earth is named, that He would grant you, according to the riches of His glory...to know the love of Christ which passes knowledge; that you may be filled with all the fullness of God.
>
> —EPHESIANS 3:14–19

Father God, in Jesus' name I pray...

Has your child or another child you've heard about ever experienced a special encounter with God? Record it here for future generations to read!

Before I add my closing thoughts, are there any major points or directions you've received from God while reading this book? Please share them here!

Conclusion

I'll never forget the day when this preschool mom looked up into the ceiling hoping God could see her down below and asked, "Is it really possible to actually walk in the Spirit with three wild preschoolers in the house?"

Walking in the Spirit in my house with three preschoolers became my heart's pursuit—it also brought the framework for this book.

If 75 percent of our child's character and personality will be developed by age five, we have a lot of work ahead of us! The irony is that even with all of our diligence in preschool parenting, our job is to eventually work ourselves out of a job. My greatest joy will be when my children hear and obey the Holy Spirit's voice more and more, needing less and less daily prodding from Mom and Dad.

Most parents have high hopes of seeing their child succeed in athletics, academics or music. Those things are useful, but knowing how to live life in sweet fellowship with the Spirit is the most beneficial capability that any child can possess.

I've collaborated with my publisher to give preschool parents a place to submit questions and comments. If you'd like to share your thoughts or questions, please log on to www.charismalife.com. Click on the "Contact Us" link on the lefthand side of the page. I'm sure you have some great ideas on preschool parenting that could benefit us all. Log on and share them with us!

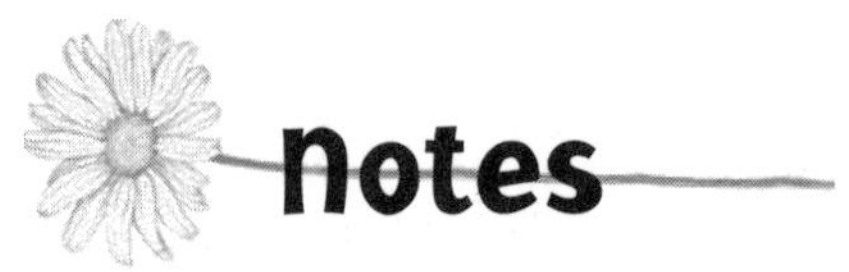

notes

Introduction

1. Peter Marshall and David Manuel, *The Light and the Glory* (Grand Rapids, MI: Fleming H. Revell, 1977), 285–286.

Chapter 4
Declare a Pajama Praise Party!

1. Sally J. Rogers, Ph.D. cited in a brochure prepared by the American Music Conference in consultation with Frank R. Wilson, M.D., associate clinical professor of neurology at the University of California School of Medicine in San Francisco, and Franz L. Roehmann, Ph.D., professor of music at the University of Colorado, Denver. Dr. Wilson and Dr. Roehmann were codirectors of the 1987 Music and Child Development Conference held in Denver under the sponsorship of the Biology of Music Making, Inc.

Chapter 5
Winning the No-No War

1. Elijah House, John and Paula Sanford, 1000 S. Richards Rd., Post Falls, ID 83854.
2. Diana Baumrind, Ph.D., "Does causally relevant research support a blanket injunction against the use of disciplinary spanking?" Address to the annual convention of the American Psychological Association, San Francisco, CA, 2001.
3. Marshall and Manuel, *The Light and the Glory,* 285.

Chapter 6
The Law Is a Teacher

1. Kenneth N. Taylor and Annabel Spenceley, *The Bible in Pictures for Little Eyes* (Chicago, IL: Moody Press, 1997).
2. Kenneth N. Taylor, Richard Hook and Frances Hook, *My First Bible in Pictures* (Wheaton, IL: Tyndale, 1990).

Chapter 7
Sibling Rivalry

1. Florence Littauer, *Silver Boxes: The Gift of Encouragement* (Dallas, TX: Word Publishing, 1989).

Chapter 12
When My Child Needs Healing

1. Paul C. Reisser and James C. Dobson, *The Focus on the Family Complete Book on Baby and Child Care* (Wheaton, IL: Tyndale House, 1999).
2. Phyllis F. Balch, C.N.C. and James F. Balch, M.D., *Prescription for Nutritional Healing* (New York: Avery Penguin Putnam, 2000).

Chapter 13
Preparing for School

1. C. Hope Flinchbaugh, *Daughter of China* (Bloomington, MN: Bethany House Publishers, 2002).
2. Carol Antoinette Peacock and Shawn Costello Brownell, *Mommy Far, Mommy Near* (Morton Grove, IL: Albert Whitman & Co., 2000).
3. For more information see www.family.org.

Chapter 14
Choosing a School

1. Dorothy Sayers, "The Lost Tools of Learning," copyrighted by National Review, 150 East 35th St., New York, NY 10016. (For more information, see www.gbt.org/text/sayers.)
2. Maria Montessori, *The Secret of Childhood,* reissue edition (New York: Ballantine Books, 1992).
3. Alvin Rosenfeld, M.D., Nicole Wise and Robert Coles, *The Over-Scheduled Child: Avoiding the Hyper-Parenting Trap* (New York: St. Martin's Press, Griffin Trade Paperbacks, 2001).
4. Reisser and Dobson, *The Focus on the Family Complete Book of Baby and Child Care,* 405–406.

Chapter 16
Children Yielded to the Spirit

1. David Walters, *Children Aflame* (Macon, GA: Good News Fellowship Ministries, 1996).
2. Ibid.
3. David Walters, personal conversation.

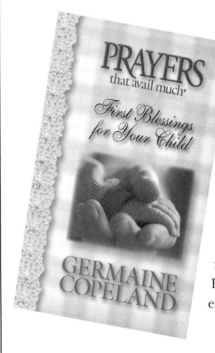